I0120367

De Vincent Collection of American Sheet Music

The National Minstrel Folio

Containing a Splendid Selection of Ballads, Comic and Sentimental Song...

De Vincent Collection of American Sheet Music

The National Minstrel Folio
Containing a Splendid Selection of Ballads, Comic and Sentimental Song...

ISBN/EAN: 9783744784375

Printed in Europe, USA, Canada, Australia, Japan

THE

NATIONAL MINSTREL FOLIO.

Containing a Splendid Selection of

Ballads, Comic and Sentimental Songs.

Plantation Melodies, &c., &c.,

PUBLISHED BY

NATIONAL MUSIC CO.,

CHICAGO, ILL.

New York: BENJ. W. HITCHCOCK, 385 Sixth Avenue

Contents of the National Minstrel Folio.

		Page
BLACK EYED BESSIE LYLE	Walker	77
BY THE OLD WILLOW TREE IN THE GLEN	Cranmer	64
CHINESE, THE CHINESE YOU KNOW	Mullaly	86
COONS ARE ON PARADE	Lewis	5
DANDY SERVANTS	Brigham	80
DEAR LOVE, A SWEET GOOD NIGHT	Jenks	92
DE GOLDEN CHARIOT	Brigham	28
DE GOSPEL BELLS AM SOUNDING	Majors	20
DEY STOLE MY CHILD AWAY	Kavanaugh	96
DUBLIN BAY	Barker	44
ELSIE DARLING, I AM WAITING	Cox	83
FLIRT THE	Carleton	40
FUN WITH THE BOYS	Lampard	138
GIRL ON ROLLER SKATES	Lewis	134
HE GETS THERE JUST THE SAME	Langey	72
HE WAS A CARELESS MAN	Grossmith	118
HOW'S YOUR SISTER MARY?	Robinson	74
HURRAH FOR COMPANY B	Brigham	108
IN THE MORNING BY THE SUNLIGHT	Lewis	23
I'SE GWINE TO GET HOME BIMEBY	Sawyer	56
ITS PROPER, QUITE PROPER, YOU KNOW	Brigham	8
JANIE	Walker	90
JAPANESE LOVE SONG	Dick	68
JERUSALEM ROAD	Lewis	126
LILLIAN, I WAIT FOR THEE	Brigham	103
LITTLE FISHER MAIDEN	Waldman	61
LITTLE SWEETHEART SAY GOOD BYE	Sawyer	115
LULLABY, FROM ERMINIE	Jacobowski	38
MAID OF THE MILL	Adams	47
MAMMA'S CHILD	Carleton	158
MARGARETHA	Jenks	152
MY BEWITCHING NELL	Johnsen	26
MY LORD IS WRITIN' DOWN TIME	Sawyer	144
PRETTY DIMPLED CHEEKS	Hogan	12
PRETTY LIPS	Lloyd	141
RING DEM CHIMIN' BELLS	Sawyer	124
ROCKING THE BABY TO SLEEP	Brigham	34
SLEEP BABY SLEEP	Handley	58
SONGS THAT MOTHER SUNG	Compton	132
STOP DAT KNOCKING AT DE DOOR	Winnemore	148
STROLLING BY THE BROOKLET	Pallma	31
SWEET BE YOUR DREAMS LOVE	Skelly	16
SWEET KITTIE CLOVER	Kean	146
THEY ALL LOVE JACK	Adams	50
TRIP TO THE COUNTRY	Mann	106
VILLAGE PEDDLER	Garibaldi	112
WHEN E'ER I SEE THOSE SMILING EYES	Magill	120
WHERE THE MORNING GLORIES TWINE	Winchell	129
WILL YOU MISS ME WHEN I'M GONE	Sawyer	53
YES I'LL BE DAR	Sawyer	100
YOU'LL SOMETIMES THINK OF ME	Coote	154

THE COONS ARE ON PARADE.

Words and Music By
DAN LEWIS

Arranged By
LOUIS BODECKER

Tempo di March.

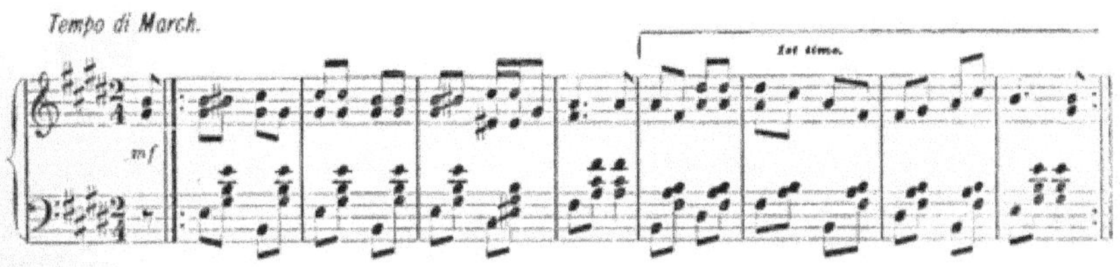
mf
1st time.

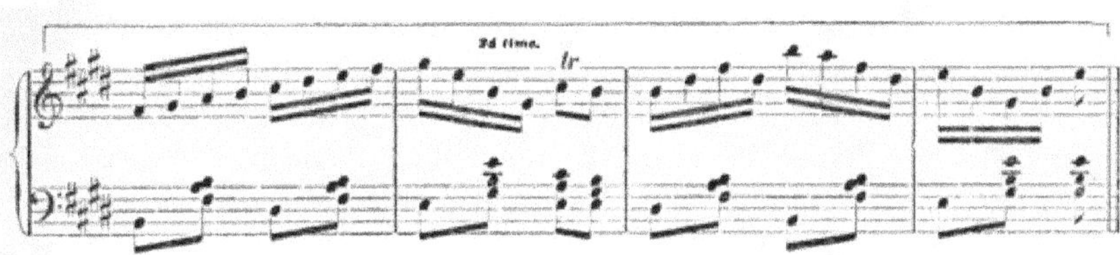
2d time.
tr

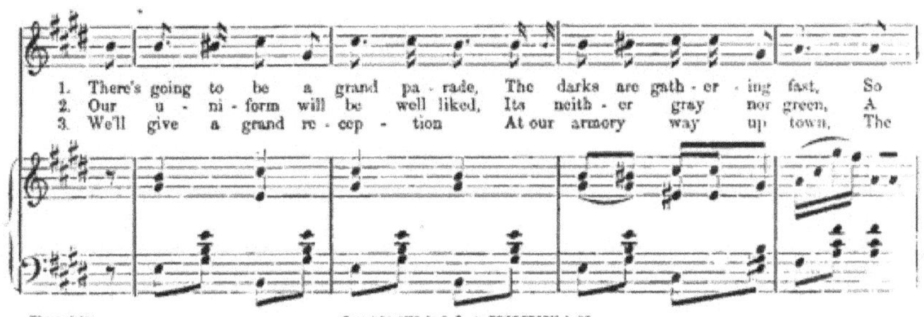
1. There's going to be a grand pa - rade, The darks are gath - er - ing fast, So
2. Our u - ni - form will be well liked, Its neith - er gray nor green, A
3. We'll give a grand re - cep - tion At our armory way up town, The

get your stand and you can see When we go march - ing past, You
nav - y blue with yel - low stripes, The fin - est ev - er seen, You
sup - per will be con - duct - ed by The wife of Cap - tain Brown, The

saw the seventh, you have seen the ninth, And oth - er white brig - ades, You
all should hear the mus - ic, How nice it will be played By the
hall ni - ce - ly dec - o - rat - ed, The ta - ble grand - ly laid, The

bet us coons will high - ly loom, While out up - on pa - rade.
col - or - ed band that leads us coons, While out up - on pa - rade.
way things was eat we'll nev - er for - get, When the coons came off pa - rade.

Hip, hip, hur - rah, you'll hear them say, As we go march - ing by. The
la - dies from the wind - ows, With their handkerchiefs wav - ing high............ The
yel - low girls on the side - walk, Pun - ish - - ing lem - on - ade, And
mash - ing all the dan - dy coons, While out up - on pa - rade......

It's Proper, Quite Proper You Know.

A TOPICAL SONG.

Words by George LeRoy. Music by G. B. BRIGHAM.

Tempo di Valse.
1. Odd styles An - glo - ma - ni - ac's of - ten af - fect, It's prop - er, quite
2. The suits that we see are quite fan - cy this fall, They're prop - er, quite
3. Young men to the bal - let per form - an - ces go, It's prop - er, quite
4. The church oys - ter sup - per is now a good show, It's prop - er, quite
prop - er you know, ... No mat - ter how ug - ly, no
prop - er you know, ... And some are so loud you can
prop - er you know, ... They're all so near - sight - ed they
prop - er you know, ... The youths and the dam - sels in

one will ob - ject It's prop - er, quite prop - er you know, ... The
most hear em call, But prop - er, quite prop - er you know, ... The
want the front row, It's prop - er, quite prop - er you know, ... Then
cou - ples all go. It's prop - er, quite prop - er you know, ... The
canes the swells car - ry are too big for toys, The mus - cu - lar
plaids are too gor - geous for me too ex - press, But the size of
one falls in love with some girl on the stage, In - vites her to
crowds to the fes - ti - val read - i - ly troop, And all gath - er
ex - er - cise no dude en - joys, And they'll soon have them carried for
the squares you can readi - ly guess, When you need a whole suit to play
sup - per, then fan - cy his rage, When he finds that she e - quals
round in a most anx - ions group, To draw lots for the oyster that's

them by small boys, It's prop - er, quite prop - er you know. . . .
one game of chess, It's prop - er, quite prop - er you know. . . .
his grandmother's age, It's prop - er, quite prop - er you know. . . .
lost "in the soup, It's prop - er, quite prop - er you know. . . .

Chorus.

Oh, yes, it's prop - er, ... prop - er, It's

prop - er, quite prop - er you know, Oh, yes, it's

pro - per . . . it's pro - per, quite pro - per you know. . . . . .

5 A great deal of talk just at present is rife,
It's proper, quite proper you know,
About what is called the "elixir of life,"
It's proper, quite proper you know,
If there's anything in it, we all must confess,
That it surely will bring a great deal of distress
To those gilded youth who rich uncles possess;
It's proper, quite proper you know.

6 Drop a dime in the slot when you go to a play;
It's proper, quite proper you know,
And you'll find a neat op'ra glass waiting straightway,
It's proper, quite proper you know,
They'll soon have things fixed so that anyone can
Just drop in a dime and a flask he will scan
That will save you a trip out, for seeing a man;
'Twill be proper, quite proper you know.

7 They say that the bustle is now out of style;
It isn't quite proper you know,
The thin girls don't like it; but stout girls all smile;
It's proper, quite proper you know,
Now what has become of the bustle you ask,
To answer that surely is not a hard task,
It makes for small brothers a fine base-ball mask;
It's proper, quite proper you know,

8 There will be a World's fair in three years or so,
It's proper, quite proper you know.
It now is a question just where it will go,
There's lots of towns proper you know,
I doubt very much as to which place is best
But I think that this plan is well worthy a test
Let's have two World's Fairs, one down east, one out west;
That's proper, quite proper you know.

9 The girls of to-day are a curious lot,
But proper, quite proper you know,
Their question is ever, "how much has he got,"
That's proper, quite proper you know,
To bright young Americans no chance affords,
But heiresses who have of their money in hoards
Will pay fancy prices for earls, dukes and lords·
It's proper, quite proper you know.

654 It's Proper, Quite Proper. 4-4.

Pretty Dimpled Cheeks.

By WILL. H. HOGAN.

INTRODUCTION.
Waltz tempo.
rit.
p a tempo.
mf
mf
p rit. tempo.
1. Oft when the twi - light deep - ens slow o'er the lea, I de - light in
2. And when the moon - light gleams from o - ver the hills. Thoughts of her it
p rit.
tempo.
dreams Of a maid - en who's all the world to me, The fair-est of
brings, And her voice my heart with sweet mu - sic fills, When ev - er the

all she seems, Once more I hear her ten-der re-plies,
night bird, sings, And star-light speaks to me of her eyes
As in dreams she speaks,........ And in vis-ions I see her smil-ing
Beam-ing in-to mine......... As so gent-ly gleaming in sum-mer
mf
p
eyes, And pret-ty dim-ple cheeks....... Although she is far a-
skies, Ra-di-ant ev-er they shine....... But I hear a step ap-
-way from me, Yet in spir-it a-gain we meet........ I will sail a-
-proach me now, And a sweet voice rings on my ear......... 'Tis my own true

rit.
tempo.
-way a-cross the sea, My lit-tle sweet-heart to greet. Ah, the sweet-est
love who comes I trow, Bringing me sol-ace and cheer, Yes, 'tis she whose
rit.
thought of mem-o-ry this, That my fond heart seeks,........ That a-gain I'll
faith-ful heart had grown sad, Wait-ing o'er the sea,.......... So to meet me,
mf
p
CHORUS.
meet her and fond-ly kiss Her pret-ty dim-pled cheeks...... Well I
greet me, and make me glad. She has at last come to me.........
know that she'll be true,........ Yes, what-ev-er may be-
p

-tide. . . . . . . Soon a - cross the o - cean blue, I'll go to claim my fair bride, . . .
. . And I hear her fond re - plies, ... As in dreams she soft - ly speaks, ...
Eyes brightly beam - ing shine thro' my dream - ing, And pret-ty dim - pled cheeks.
CODA.
D.S.
rit.

Sweet be Your Dreams, Love.

SONG.

Words and Music by J. P. SKELLY.

Allegretto.
mf
1. The
2. Oh!
3. Then
hour is late and we must part, 'Tis hard to say "good - bye,".......... But
say that soon we'll meet a - gain, Our ten - der love to share,.......... In
breathe a - gain in pre - cious words, Your heart's true, lov - ing vow........... Your

safe with you I leave my heart—You know its in - most sigh. 'Tis
ab - sence there is on - ly pain, That no fond heart can bear. Your
voice is sweet - er than the birds That sing from bough to bough. Oh!

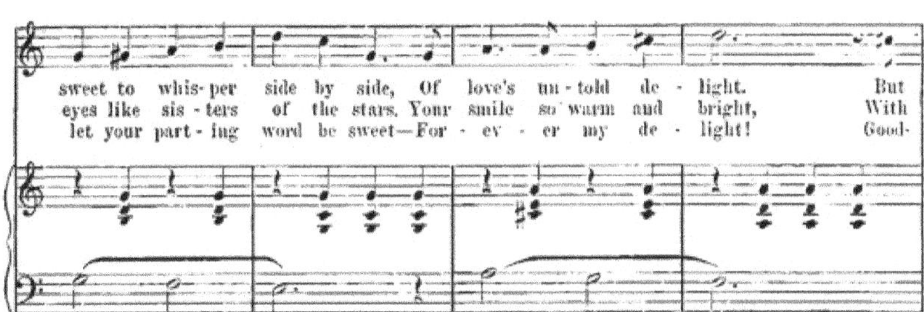
sweet to whis - per side by side, Of love's un - told de - light. But
eyes like sis - ters of the stars, Your smile so warm and bright, With
let your part - ing word be sweet—For - ev - er my de - light! Good-

poco rit.
moments fly, once more good bye. Sweet be your dreams to - night.
light di - vine up - on me shine, Sweet be your dreams to - night.
bye, my own, in si - lence lone, Sweet be your dreams to - night.
poco rit.

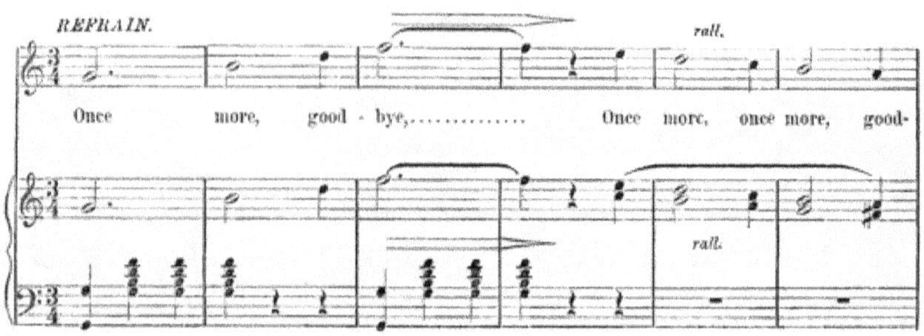
REFRAIN.
rall.
Once more, good - bye,.............. Once more, once more, good-
rall.

p Tempo di Valse.
bye.......... Sweet be your dreams, love. When slum - ber
p

veils your eyes............. Bright vis ions greet..... you, Of

fu - ture par - a - dise......... And while you are dream -

ing, In all your beau - ty beam - - ing, Call back these

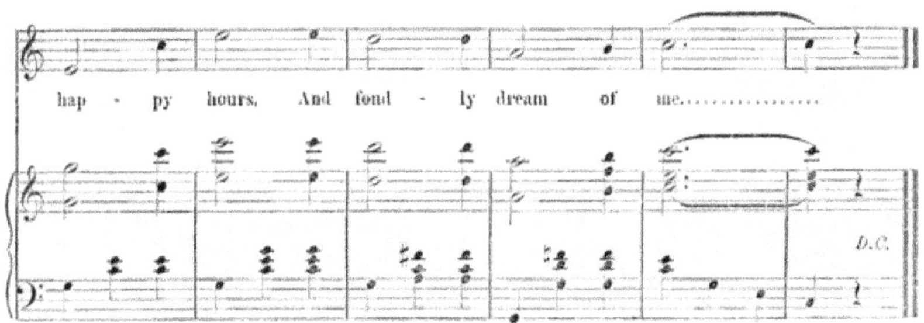
hap - py hours, And fond - ly dream of me.................
D.C.

De Gospel Bells am Sounding.

JUBILEE SOLO AND CHORUS.

Words and Music by George W. Major.

Moderato.

8va

f

CHORUS.

1. De Gos - pel bell am sound - ing, Sound - ing, am sound - ing. De
2. De Gos - pel lamp am shi - ning, Shi - ning, am shi - ning. De
3. De Gos - pel horn am blow - ing, Blow - ing, am blow - ing. De

p

Gos - pel bell am sound - ing. Oh, hear it ring! Can't you hear it ring? De
Gos - pel lamp am shi - ning. Oh, see it shine! Can't you see it shine? De
Gos - pel horn am blow - ing. Oh, hear it blow! Can't you hear it blow? De

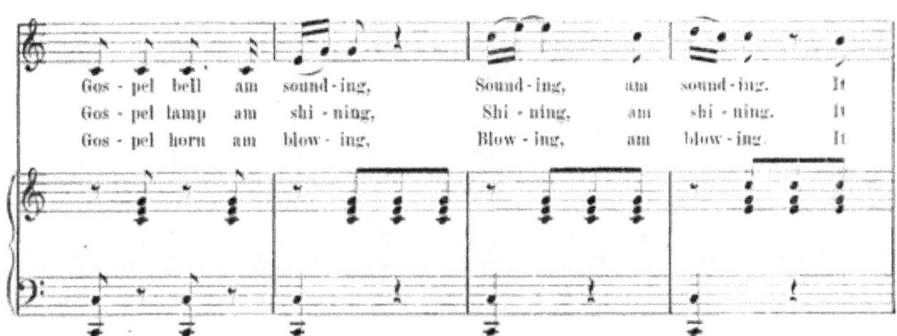
Gos - pel bell am sound - ing, Sound - ing, am sound - ing. It
Gos - pel lamp am shi - ning, Shi - ning, am shi - ning. It
Gos - pel horn am blow - ing, Blow - ing, am blow - ing. It

sounds so sweet I al - ways love To hear dem gos - pel bells.
shines so bright I al - ways love To see dat gos - pel light.
blows so loud dat eb - 'ry coon Can hear dat gos - pel horn.
dim.

Solo.
Chorus.
Oh, lit - tle chil - dren hear dat sound! Hear dat sound, gath - er 'round.
Oh, lit - tle chil - dren see dat light, Shi - ning bright throught the night.
Oh, lit - tle chil - dren hear it's song, Ring - ing out, clear and strong.
p
unison.

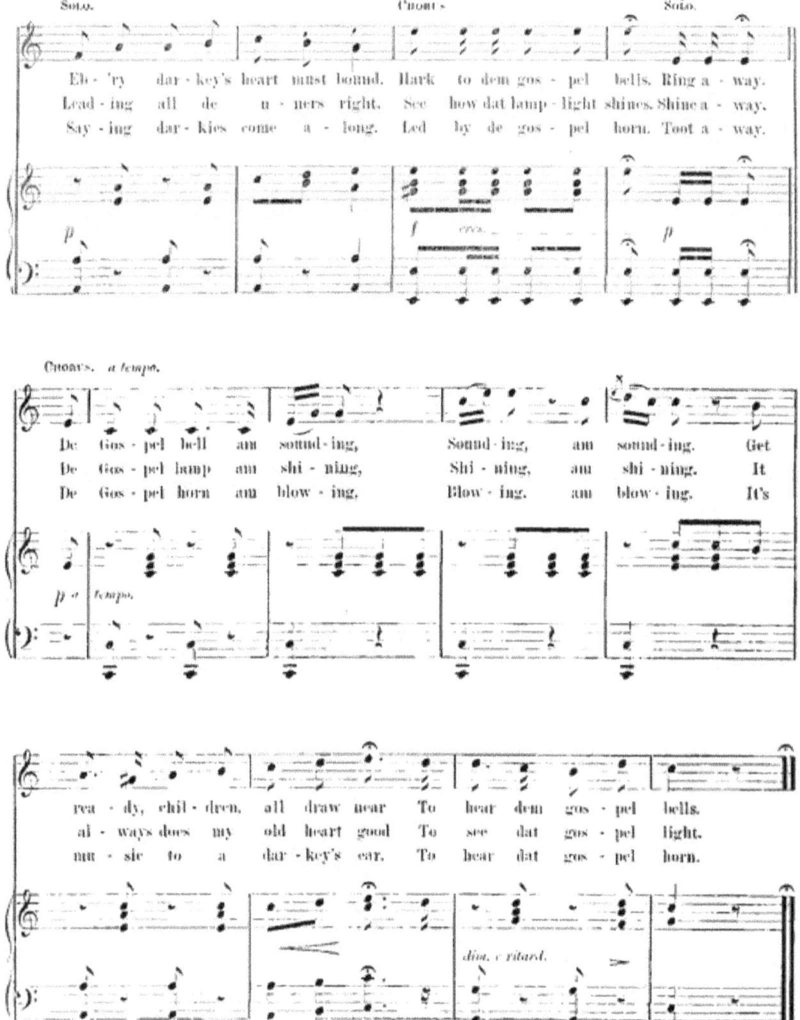
Solo.
Chorus.
Solo.
Eb - 'ry dar - key's heart must bound. Hark to dem gos - pel bells. Ring a - way.
Lead - ing all de - u - ners right. See how dat lamp - light shines. Shine a - way.
Say - ing dar - kies come a - long. Led by de gos - pel horn. Toot a - way.
cres.
Chorus. a tempo.
De Gos - pel bell am sound - ing, Sound - ing, am sound - ing. Get
De Gos - pel lamp am shi - ning, Shi - ning, am shi - ning. It
De Gos - pel horn am blow - ing, Blow - ing, am blow - ing. It's
a tempo.
rea - dy, chil - dren, all draw near To hear dem gos - pel bells.
al - ways does my old heart good To see dat gos - pel light.
mu - sic to a dar - key's ear. To hear dat gos - pel horn.
dim. e ritard.

In the Morning by the Sunlight.

WORDS AND MUSIC BY
DAN LEWIS.

ARRANGED BY
LOUIS BODECKER.

Moderato.
Introduction
1st time p
2d time f

tr
tr
1st time.
2d time.

1. In the morn - ing by the sun-light, When the day is bright and clear...... I
2. So when your work is o - ver, Go and brush up your sun - day clothes.... And
3. The ta - ble will be laid out, With ev' - ry - thing that's sweet.... And
p

want you col - ored peo - ple Sure - ly to be there, Put the
tell the lit - tle chil - dren To let the old folks know, Then stop
when they blow their trum - pet, You can all sit down and eat, Par - son
har - ness on the mule, And hitch him to the cart........ I
in at old aunt Chloe, Un - cle Pete and Par - son Brown, ... For
Brown will give a lec - - ture, Pick - a min - ies they will dance...... Aunt
prom - ised to be there, So I'll make an ear - ly start....
they have all got tick - ets and They sure - ly will come down....
Han - nah she'll get up and sing, Buck and Wing - ing by Suse and Nance.
CHORUS.
Every - thing will be all right, So I want you all to come, And
tr
tr

Han-nah she will be there too, And have the 'pos-sum done........ You might bring the lit - tle
children, If the moon is shin - ing bright, For I've got to get there early, Yes, In the morning by the sunlight.
DANCE.
1st time p
2d time f

MY BEWITCHING NELL.

Words by VOLKMAR JOHNSEN.

Music Arr. by EMIL BECKER.

Allegretto.
dance.
FINE
1. Look yonder, where the laughing, babbling brook Skips o'er the pebbles like a
shades of evening lin - ger when they meet, To weave a spell a-round this
fair - y, There stands a lit - tle cot, a love - ly nook, The fin - est on the prairie, The
bower, Where dwells a blue eyed maid - en, pure and sweet, The fair - est prairie

flower. I love her, I love her, My se - cret I must tell.
f

D.S. al Fine.
My be - witch - ing Nell.
ff
D.S. al Fine.

2. Around the lattice creeps the blushing rose,
 The ivy to the wall is clinging,
Beneath the roof the birds, in sweet repose,
 Their lays of love are singing;
I see the blushing roses come and go,
 I feel the twining ivy tremble,
I hear the lays of love, I see the glow
 That can no more dissemble:
She loves me, she loves me, my secret I must tell.
  My bewitching Nell

3. The little stars are twinkling on their way,
 The moon moves on in silent splendor,
The zephyrs with my darling's ringlets play,
 And whisper words so tender;
I watch the zephyrs in their airy flight,
 I kiss those golden, glowing tresses,
I see two little stars so pure and bright
 —My love her love confesses,
I'm happy, I'm happy, no words my joy can tell.
  My bewitching Nell.

Dedicated to my friend, S. P. CANTWELL, Bass, Alpine Quartette.

DE GOLDEN CHARIOT.

Words and Music by GUS. B. BRIGHAM.

INTRODUCTION.

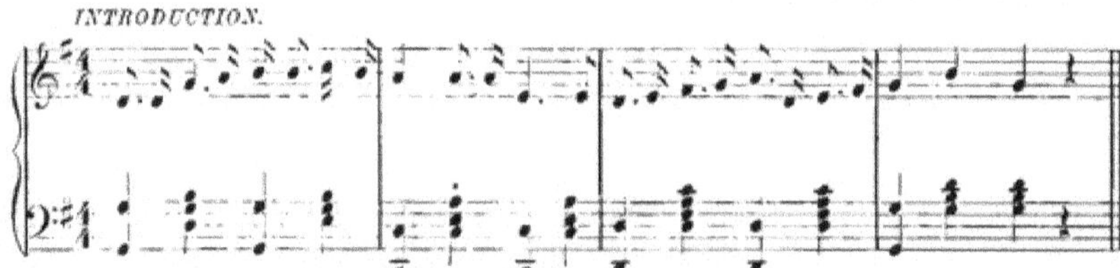

1. Sail-in down de rib-er, at de close of de day, I hear de an-gels call-ing for de
2. You can not get to hea-ven by look-ing at de sky, And wond-'rin why de an-gels al-ways

chil-dren to pray, To hur-ry up a pout-en, and to hoe de field of corn, As de
pass you by, If you will sing and shout at de broke ob de dawn. Why de

gold - en chariot's a com - in in de morn, Fo de bells are all a ring - in, and I
gold - en chariot will take you in de morn. Den go and tell old mas - sa dat youse
8va.
Bells.
Bell.

know dey ring fo me, Kase good old mas - sa told me, "sure's your born!" Put
gwine a - way wid me. I know dey'll pass you in as sure's your born! Put
8va.
Bells.
Bells.

on your gold-en slippers fo de good Lord to see, And to ride up in de char-iot in de morn.

CHORUS. First time f second time pp
1st TENOR.
Den I hear de an - gels, hear de an - gels call, I know deys call-in fo, call - in loud fo me. Put
2d TENOR.
Den I hear de an - gels call, I know deys call-in fo me. Put
1st BASS.
Den I hear de an - gels, hear de an - gels call, I know deys call-in fo, call - in loud fo me. Put
2d BASS.
know deys a call-in fo, call - in loud fo me. Put

Repeat pp
on your gold-en slip-pers, to climb de gold-en stair. Gold-en chariot youse gwine to ride wid me.
on your gold-en slip-pers, to climb de gold-en stair. In de Gold-en chariot youse gwine to ride wid me.
on your gold-en slip-pers, to climb de gold-en stair. Gold-en chariot youse gwine to ride wid me.

STROLLING BY THE BROOKLET.

Words by KIRTLAND CALHOUN. *Music by* FRANK PALLMA.

p. Second time ff.
1st time.
2d time.
Strolling out the o - ther ev' - ning, Sun-set lighted every hill and
Day by day more and more I loved her, Her sweet face is ever lit with
One sum - mers eve at last I met her, Just be - side the farm - house
p
dale There I met a charming little mai - den, Im - merging from the shadow of the
smiles, And her eyes in their purity and brightness, Are but mirrors of a heart pure as a
gate, There I told her how deeply I did love her, And her answer made my happiness com

vale. I asked her if I might see her home, And laughingly she toss'd her head and
childs. Like the brook that flows by the hill - side, Ever constant in its flight toward the
plete. Some day we'll both be wed - - ded, And to - gether arm in arm we'll stroll a -
rall.
ad lib.
said, You're a stranger kind sir un - to me, To walk alone I'm not at all a -
sea, So my heart with the love that I bear her, In its flight to her shall ever constant
way, We will walk by the side of the brook-let, When the sun behind the hill bids all good -
rall.
ad lib.
CHORUS.
fraid.
be. She has won my heart With her win - ning ways,
day.
f
f
p
f

Of-ten think I of our meeting, By the side of the run - ning
p
brook Often have I strolled by that mea-dow, Just for one sweet par - ting look.
rall.
rall.
DANCE.
p

ROCKING THE BABY TO SLEEP.

Revised and arr. by C. L. KECK.

Words and Music by GUS. B. BRIGHAM.

Introduction.
8va.
1. When com - ing from toil in the eve - ning, ... You
2. When he wakes you up in the morn - ing. . . . . . . His
3. He's al - ways con - tent with his play - things, ... He
greet your dear wife with a kiss. . . . . You pick up your sweet lit - tle
face you will find a big frown, . . You laugh and you make fac - es
builds up his hous - es and halls, . . . If sis - ter should knock them all

fond - ling, . . . And think of his in - no - cent bliss, ... You
at him; . . . While robed in his lit - tle white gown, ... You
o - ver, . . . You'll make up your mind that he squalls, ... He'll
look at his fat cheeks and dim - ples, ... You chuc - kle him
dress him and take him a rid - ing, ... In his coupe, the
build them a - gain for his ma - ma, ... And when he calls
un - der the chin, ... And play with him till he gets
kind of his kin, ... And af - ter you've hugged him and
pa - pa to see, ... He tum - bles them down and then

sleep - y, ... And sing him to sleep, you be - gin. . . . . .
kissed him; . . . In your arms you take him a - gain. . . . . .
gig - gles, . . . Then "Pop" takes him up on his knee. . . . . .

CHORUS.

Rock - ing the ba - by to sleep, ... Rock - ing the

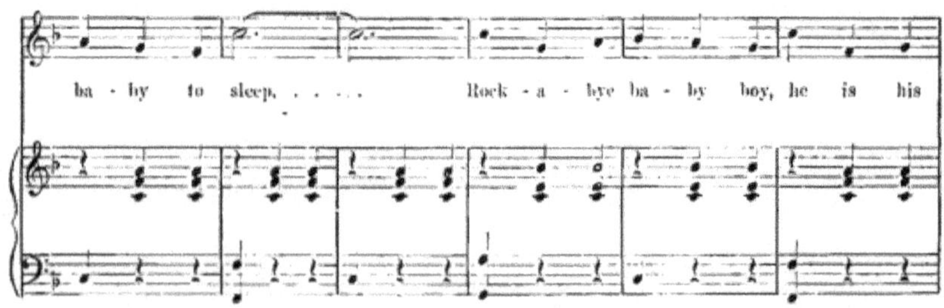
ba - by to sleep, ... Rock - a - bye ba - by boy, he is his

ritard.
moth - er's joy, Rock - ing the ba - by, the sweet lit - tle ba by boy,
Rock - ing the ba - by to sleep, ... Rock - ing the
ba - by to sleep. . . . . He is his moth - er's joy,
ritard.
Rock - a - bye ba - by boy, Rock - ing the ba - by to sleep. . . . .

LULLABY.

From "ERMINIE."

ED. JACOBOWSKI.

Moderato.

f p p

1. Dear moth - er, in dreams I see her, With lov'd face, sweet and calm, And hear her voice With love rejoice, When nestling on her arm. I think how she soft - ly press'd me, Of the tears in each glist-ning eye As her watch she'd keep, When she rock'd to sleep Her child with this lul-la - by Bye, bye, bye, bye, bye,

2. Ah! e'en when her life was eb-bing, Her words were all of me, My fu - ture years Were all her tears, Her fate was not to see. My fa - ther, I heard you weep-ing, As in sor-row you stand-ing by, And my moth - er's plaint, In her ac - cents faint, This tender, sweet lul-la - by, Bye, bye, bye, bye, bye,

mf

p
p L'istesso tempo.
bye, bye, bye, bye, bye, bye, bye, bye, bye.
Bye, bye, drow-si-ness o'er-tak-ing. Pret-ty lit-tle eye-lids
sleep Bye, bye, watch-ing till thou'rt wak - ing. Dar-ling, be thy slum - ber deep!
mf
Bye bye, drow-si-ness o'er-tak - ing, Pret-ty lit-tle eye - lids sleep. Bye, bye,
rall. dim. pp
watching till thou'rt wak-ing, Darling, be thy slum-bers deep! bye, bye bye, bye.

THE FLIRT.

SONG AND DANCE.

By GEO. M. CARLETON.

Tempo di Schottische.

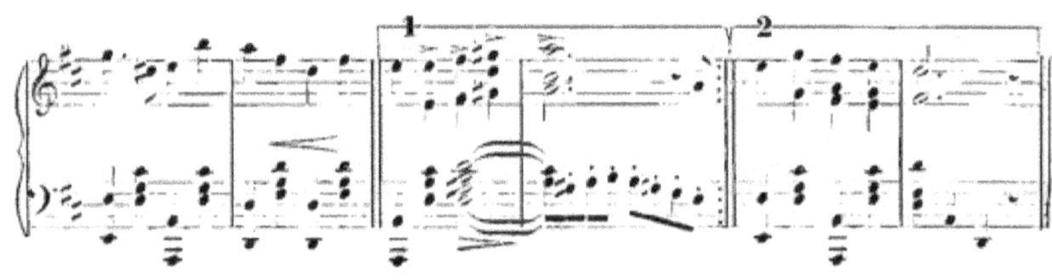

1. Oh, once while I was strolling down the street A pret - ty lit - tle charmer I did
2. We've nev - er known an - oth - er love since then We nev - er-more shall sep - a - rate a -
f
p

meet. I glanced and smiled, she did the same, Of course I bow'd my
gain. We are so hap - py, light and free. Our sor - rows all have

head. And then we spoke, she took my arm, And this is what she
fled. And oft - ten speak of when we met, And the first thing that she

said: Oh, don't you think that you're a lit - tle fresh.

I said to her, My dar - ling, don't be rash.
ff

Then we walked and talked, un - til the moon came out. Then to a park we
Now we've vis it - ed all the old fa - mil - iar spots, And the park when first we

went. And by the moonlight's silv'ry rays, So hap - py were the hours we spent.
went. Will dream in si - lence ev - er-more, Of the man - y happy hours we spent.

CHORUS.
For we would sing, And we would dance. Her laugh was light and gay. And
then in each oth - ers' compa - ny we whiled the i - dle hours a - way.
DANCE.

DUBLIN BAY.

Words by Mrs. CRAWFORD. Music by GEO. BARKER.

1. They sail'd a - way in a gal - lant bark, Roy Neal and his fair young
2. Three days they sail'd when a storm a - rose, And the Light - 'ning swept the deep,

bride, They had ven - tur'd all in that bound - ing ark, That
deep, When the thun - der crash broke the short re - pose Of the
danc'd on the sil - v'ry tide; Roy Neal, he clasp'd his
wea - ry sea - boy's sleep, Roy Neal, he clasp'd his
weep - ing bride, and he kiss'd the tears a - way, And he
weep - ing bride, and he kiss'd the tears a - way, O,
Watch'd the shore re - cede from sight Of his own sweet "Dub - lin Bay."
love 'twas a fear - ful hour, he cried, When we left sweet "Dub - lin Bay."

3. On the crowd - ed deck of that doom - ed ship, Some fell in their mad de -
- spair, But some more calm, with a ho - lier lip, Sought the God of the storm in
pray'r; "She has struck on a rock," the sea - men cried, In the breath of their wild dis -
- may, And the ship went down with that fair young bride, That sail'd from "Dub - lin Bay."
rall.

THE MAID OF THE MILL.

Words by HAMILTON AÏDÉ. | Music by STEPHEN ADAMS.

Andante grazioso.
Cantabile.
1. Gold-en years a - go in a mill be-side the sea, There dwelt a lit - tle maid - en, who
2. Lead-en years have past, grey - hair'd I look a - round: The earth has no such maidens now, such
plight - ed her faith to me; The mill-wheel now is si - lent, the
mill - wheels turn not round. But when - e'er I think of Heav'n, and of

maid's eyes closed be; And all that now re-mains of her, are the words she sang to me.
what the an-gels be, I see a-gain that lit-tle maid, and hear her words to me.
mf
p
rall.
Tempo di Valse, e con dolcezza.
"Do not for-get me! Do not for-get me! Think
p dolce.
some-times of me still.
poco più mosso.
When the morn
breaks, and the thros-tle a-wakes, Re-mem-ber the maid
cres.

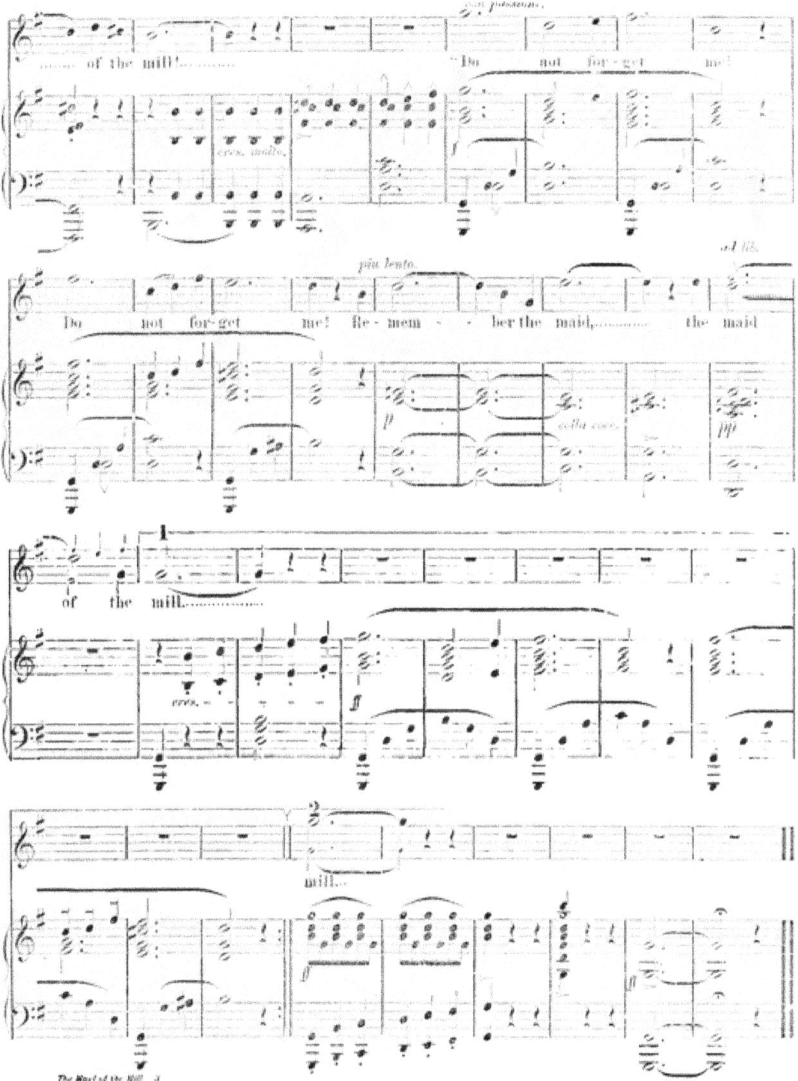
of the mill!
"Do not for-get me!
cres. molto.
più lento.
ad lib.
Do not for-get me! Re-mem - ber the maid, the maid
colla voce.
of the mill.
cres.
mill.

THEY ALL LOVE JACK.

Words by F. E. WEATHERLY. | Music by STEPHEN ADAMS

With Spirit.
f
1. When the ship is trim and read-y, And the jol - ly days are
2. Where he goes their hearts go with him, E'en his ship he calls her
3. When he's sail'd the world all o - ver, And a - gain he steps a -
p
done, When the last good-byes are whisper'd, And Jack a - board is gone; The
"she;" Up a - loft that "lit - tle cher-ub" Sure a maid-en she must be. And as
shore, There are scores of lass - es wait-ing To love him all the more; He may

lass - es fall a - weep-ing, as they watch his ves - sel's track, For all the lands - men
o'er the sea he trav - els, the mermaids down be - low Would give their crys - tal
lose his gold - en guineas, but a wife he'd nev - er lack. If he'd wed them all, they'd
p
cres.
lov - ers are noth - ing af - ter Jack, For all the lands-men lov - ers are
king - doms for the love of Jack, I trow, Would give their crys - tal king - doms for the
take him, for they all love Jack! If he'd wed them all, they'd take him, for they
rall.
tempo.
noth - ing af - ter Jack,.... For his heart is like the sea, ev - er o - pen, brave and
love of Jack, I trow,.... For his heart is like the sea, ev - er o - pen, brave and
all, they all love Jack..... For his heart is like the sea, ev - er o - pen, brave and
mf

free, And the girls must lone - ly be......... Till his ship comes back; But if
love's the best of all........ That can a man be-fall,........ Why, Jack's the king of
mf
f
rall.
1st & 2d.
3d.
all...... For they all love Jack! Jack!
colla voce.
ff
ff

Will You Miss Me when I'm Gone?

Words by Harry B. Smith.

Music by Jacob J. Sawyer.

INTRODUCTION.

1. When these eyes at last are clos - - ing, And for - ev - er cease to
2. Will you tread the paths to - geth - - er, Where we wandered hand in
3. Will you come when spring is bloom - - ing, And the ferns and blos - soms

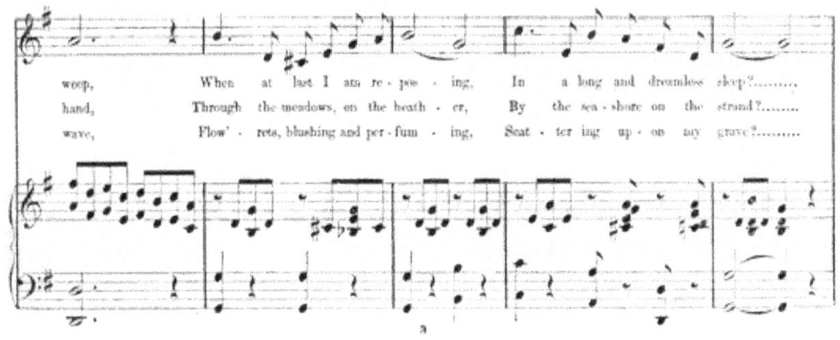
weep, When at last I am re - pos - ing, In a long and dreamless sleep?.........
hand, Through the meadows, on the heath - er, By the sea - shore on the strand?........
wave, Flow' - rets, blushing and per - fum - ing, Scat - ter ing up - on my grave?.........

Will you then my mem-'ry cher-ish, Hold-ing me, as ev-er, dear?........ Or will re-col-lec-tion
We have heard with eyes that glis-ten, Songs come waft-ed o'er the sea;........ When to them a-lone you
And will you watch for my com-ing, At the door at e-ven-tide........, When the wild bees 'round are
per-ish, When my voice you cease to hear?......... Will you think of me still faith-ful-ly,
list-en, Will you sometimes think of me?......... Will you hear the song-birds sing-ing gay?
hum-ming, And the birds sing far and wide.......... Will you watch and wait in vain for me,
In life's night as at its dawn, my darling? Will you weep for me, I won-der, Will you miss me when I'm gone?
See the flow'rets bloom in grace, my darling? With no mem-o-ry up-springing, Of a distant, vanished face?
As the wea-ry years glide on, my darling? For my foot-step will you list-en? Will you miss me when I'm gone?

CHORUS.

SOPRANO.
Will you think of me still faith - ful - ly, In life's night as at its dawn?............ Ah!
ALTO.
TENOR.
Will you think of me still faith - ful - ly, In life's night as at its dawn?............ Ah!
BASS.
PIANO.

will you weep for me, I won - der, will you miss me when I'm gone...................
gone, yes, when I'm gone.
will you weep for me, I won - der, will you miss me when I'm gone, yes, when I'm gone.

I'SE GWINE TO GET HOME BYME BYE.

JACOB J. SAWYER.

1. Go 'way, my broth - er, go 'way, Doan want you trou - ble me now; I'se got dis hon - ey-comb
2. Yes, stop and think, my brother, Be - fore you leab dis land; If it had - n't been for de
in my breast, And I'se gwine to heb'n at last. De way am dark and lone - ly, De
mer - cy of God, We'd all be dead and damned. Den take de Gos - pel Ban - ner, Put
riv-er am hard to cross; But with dis hon - ey-comb in my breast, I'll get to heben at last.
on your sword and shield, And with the cry of "glo - ry" die Fight - ing in the field.

CHORUS.
SOPRANO.
Um um um um um um my Lord, Um um um And I'se gwine to get a home byme by. Um
Unite sounds from the lips.
ALTO.
Hum
TENOR.
Hum
BASS.
ACCOMP.
Um um um um um my Lord, Um um um And I'se gwine to get a home byme by.
Hum
Hum

To PEARL.

SLEEP, BABY, SLEEP.

LULLABY.

Words and Music by JOHN J. HANDLEY.

Andante.
p
p
p

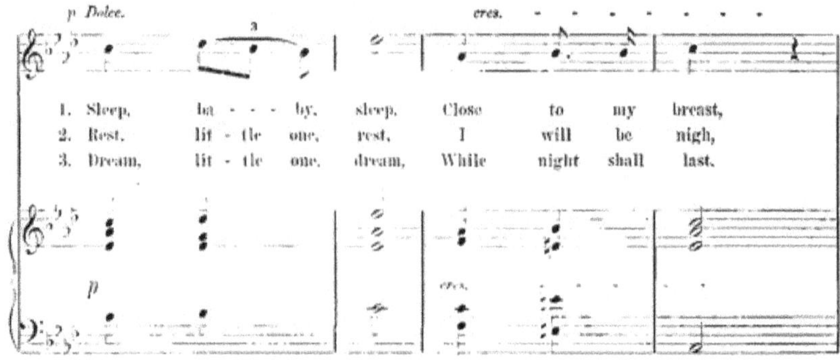
p Dolce.
cres.
1. Sleep, ba - - - by, sleep, Close to my breast,
2. Rest, lit - tle one, rest, I will be nigh,
3. Dream, lit - tle one, dream, While night shall last.
p

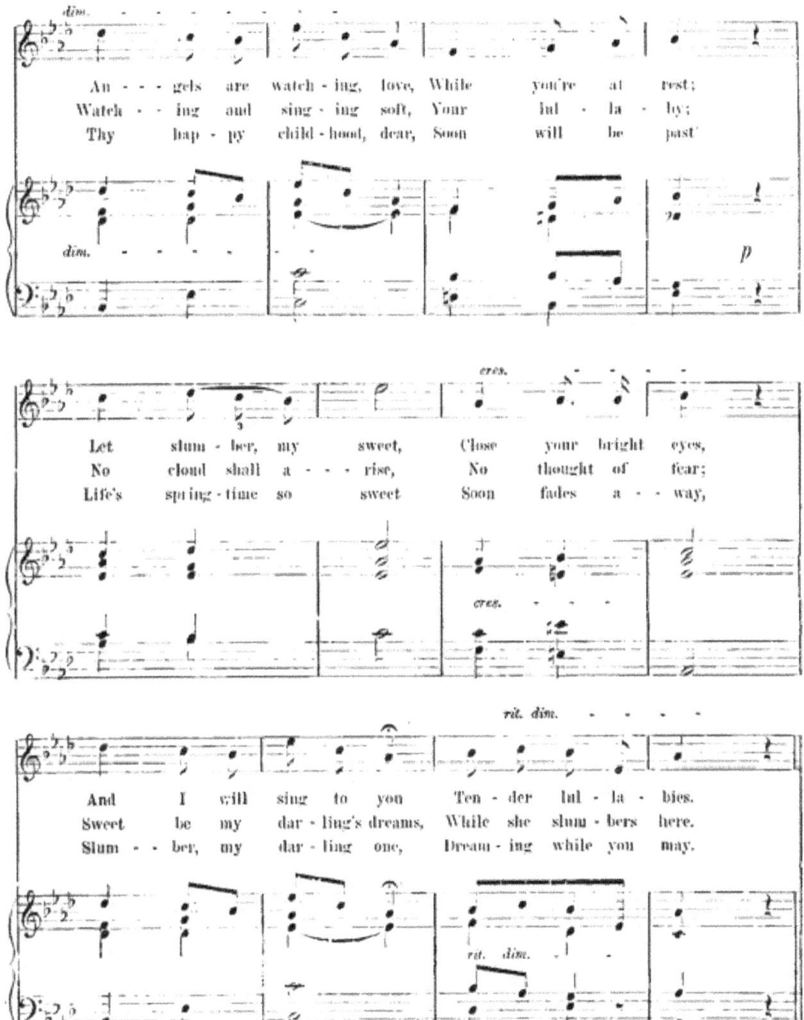
dim.
An - - - gels are watch - ing, love, While you're at rest;
Watch - - ing and sing - ing soft, Your lul - la - by;
Thy hap - py child - hood, dear, Soon will be past'
dim.
p
cres.
Let slum - ber, my sweet, Close your bright eyes,
No cloud shall a - - - rise, No thought of fear;
Life's spring - time so sweet Soon fades a - - way,
cres.
rit. dim.
And I will sing to you Ten - der lul - la - bies.
Sweet be my dar - ling's dreams, While she slum - bers here.
Slum - - ber, my dar - ling one, Dream - ing while you may.
rit. dim.

YODLE.
Tempo di Valse.
A - - - e - - o - la - e - - - - - - O - le - a - - e - du -
- - - A - le - a - e - du - ah - - - - - - A - - - - - - e - - - o -
- la e - - - - - - - - O - le - a - - e - du - ah - - oo - le - ah - - -
p
rit.
rit

THE LITTLE FISHER-MAIDEN.

DAS KLEINE FISCHERMADCHEN.

English words by GEO. BARDWELL. LUDOLF WALDMANN.

1. There was a lit - tle Fish - er - maid - - en, So love - ly and so bright, A joy un - to the sight! A joy un - to the sight! The fair - est maid in all the vil - -
1. War einst ein klei - nes Fi - - scher - mäd - - chen, So lieb - lich und so schön gar herr - lich an - zu - sehn, gar herr - lich an - zu - sehn! Die schön - ste Maid im Fi - scher - städt - -

- lage, She braved the storm - y sea, With heart so light and free, With
- chen, sie fuhr bei Sturm - ge - braus auf's wil - de Meer hin - aus, auf's
heart so light and free!.... The Mermaids came with voi - ces clear, To warn the maid of
wil - de Meer hin - aus!.... Da tauch - te auf der Nix en Schaar und warnt das Mäd - chen
a tempo.
dan - gers near! To warn the maid of dan - gers, dan - - gers near!
vor Ge fahr, und warnt das Fi - scher - mäd - chen, vor......... Ge - fahr!
a tempo.
REFRAIN.
rit.
The mer - maids' song, the mer maids' song rang long;
Der Nix - en Sang, der Niz - en Sang er - klang;
rit.

a tempo.
"Lit - tle Fish - er maid - en, Skies with storm are laid - en! Tempt no more a -
Fi - scher-in - du klei - ne, fah - re nicht al - lei - ne! fah - re nicht bei
lone the sea, Dan - ger's wait - ing there for thee! Lit - tle Fish - er maid - en
Sturm - ge-braus, auf das wil - de Meer hin-aus! Fi - scher- in du - klei - ne,
Skies with storm are la - den! Tempt no more, a - lone the sea! Dan - ger waits for thee......
fah - re nicht al - lei - ne, fah - re nicht bei Sturm-ge-braus auf das Meer hin - aus!
8va
fp
mf
Ped.

2 She cried, "all danger I am scorning!"
And laughing, on sail'd she,
Tho' wilder grew the sea,
Tho' wilder grew the sea.
Came Tritons who had heard that warning,
When these the maiden spied,
For help, for help, she cried!
For help, for help, she cried!
Her fragile boat they toss'd it o'er.
She sails the sea, alone, no more!
She threw it on the cruel, rocky shore.
REFRAIN AND CHORUS.

3 The Fisher-maiden swift was dying;
She sank beneath the wave!
But Neptune came to save!
But Neptune came to save!
Amid the tempests round them flying,
With strong and willing hand
He drew her safe to land!
He drew her safe to land!
But since that hour her joy is o'er,
She sails the sea, alone, no more.
She sails the sea, alone, alone, no more.
REFRAIN AND CHORUS.

2 Sie rief "[illegible] mich verschonen!"
Fuhr lachend durch's Gebraus
Auf's wilde Meer hinaus,
Auf's wilde Meer hinaus,
Da plötzlich tauchten auf Tritonen:
Wie die die Maid gesehn,
Da war's um sie geschehn,
Da war's um sie geschehn!
Sie packten all zu mal das Schiff
Und warfen es auf's Felsenriff,
Und schleuderten das Schiff auf's Felsenriff!
REFRAIN AND CHORUS.

3 Der Fisch'rin Nachen thät zerschellen
Da kam auf ihr Geschrei
Der Gott Neptun herbei,
Der Gott Neptun herbei!
Der führte sie durch Sturm und Wellen
Gar sicher an das Land,
Und setzt' auf den Sand,
Und setzt' auf den Sand!
Da sass die arme Fischerin,
Ihr froher Muth, er war dahin.
Ihr freier froher Muth, er war dahin.
REFRAIN AND CHORUS.

By the Old Willow Tree in the Glen.

Words by CHAS. RUSSELL. Music by WM. CRAMER.

1. When the sha - dows of eve - ning are fall - ing, And the
2. Ma - ny days I've been wait - ing to meet you, For I've
sun - light is fad - ing a - way, When a - round us the an - gel of
some - thing I'm long - ing to tell. How since we first met, in my

dark - ness Is fold - - ing her man - tle so
mem - 'ry Fond thoughts of thee al - - ways will

gray, When the whip - poor-will sings to the wil - - lows, Oh, say
swell, And in the lone hours of mid - - night, Thy

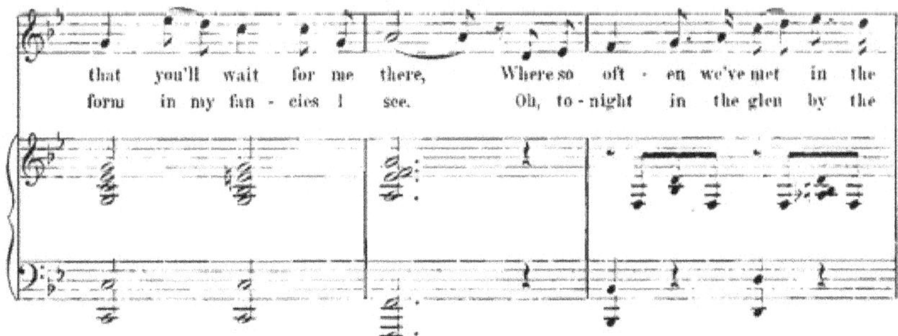
that you'll wait for me there, Where so oft - en we've met in the
form in my fan - cies I see. Oh, to-night in the glen by the

twi - - - light. By the old wil - low tree in the glen.
wil - - - - low, Tell me, dar - ling, you'll love none but me.
rit.

CHORUS.

SOPRANO.
Oh, tell me, my dar - ling, You'll love me, Be to
ALTO.
TENOR.
Tell me, my dar - ling, You'll love me, Be to
BASS.
PIANO.

rit.
me what no oth - er has been, Oh give me that promise when you
rit.
rit.
me what no oth - er has been, give me that promise when you
rit.

meet me By the old wil-low tree in the glen.
meet me By the old wil-low tree in the glen.

JAPANESE LOVE SONG.

Words by **W. Yardley.** Music by **Cotsford Dick,**

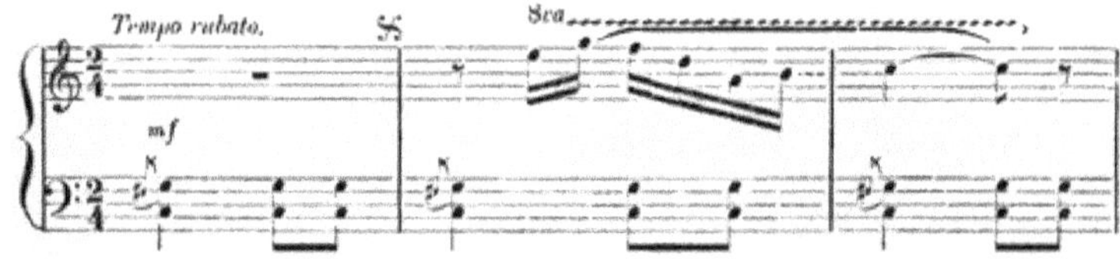
Tempo rubato.
8va
mf

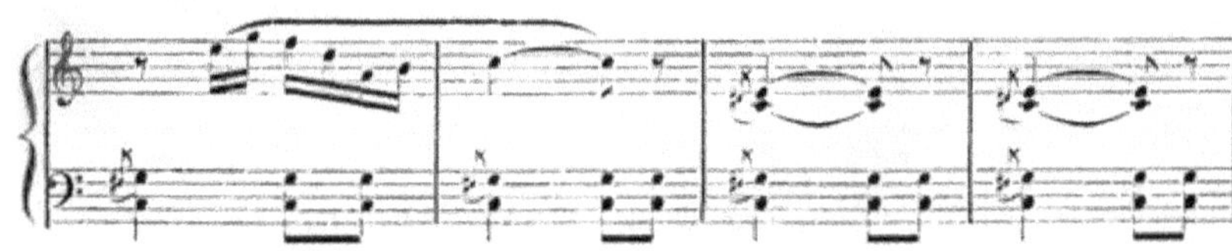

mf
1. Me once - y time a - go, Knew nice - y lit - tle man, He
2. Lit-tle miss - y, laugh - y guess. So hap - py as She am, "Ask
mf

name him self - ey Pea Cue Sin,........................ He
pap - py dear - y Chang Fi Fow,"...................... Yum
8va
lov - ey miss - y so (She call her name-y Fan) "How do - ey miss-ey well?" "Chin-
pap - py nod - dy yes, Him sweet as jol - ly jam, And ber - ry mum-my nice, Chow-
Piu lento.
Chin................ He kiss - y lit - tle miss-ey, (She
Chow.............. Um lov - ey lit - tle dove-y, I'm
8va
Piu lento.

4
a tempo.
call her name-y Fan) Lit - tle miss-ey which he love-y much-ey so, Lit - tle
duck - y lit - tle Fan, Pit - ty, pop - sy, wop - sy, tid-dy, ic - kle sing, And
miss-ey when he kiss - y, "Go a - way um naughty man," But um naughty, naughty man,
dove - y say she love - y, For her fin - ger bring a ring, For her fin - ger bring a ring,
a tempo.
p
But um naught - y, naught - y man, But um
For her fin - ger bring a ring, For her
p
Japanese Love Song.

5
naughty man a-way um would-n't go, go, go! Tip Top Whip Top
fin-ger bring a Ching a ring a ring Ching ring! Tip Top &c.
Sing So Hi, Hum Top Sing So Lo; Chip Chop Cher-ry Chop
up to the ver-y top; Tum-ble down lo Sing So. So..........
1st Ending.
Last Ending.
D. S.
Tempo, Io.

He Gets There Just the Same.

Words by WILL PETERS

Music by O. LANGEY

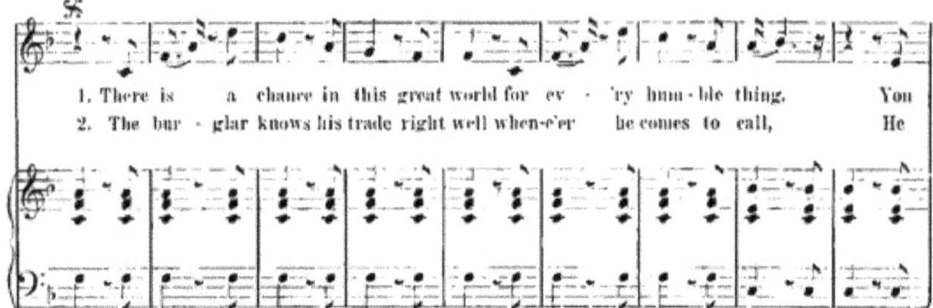
1. There is a chance in this great world for ev - 'ry hum - ble thing. You
2. The bur - glar knows his trade right well when-e'er he comes to call, He

must not judge one by his looks, as I'll pro - ceed to sing:
bur - gles all the live - long night, what - ev - er may be - fall.

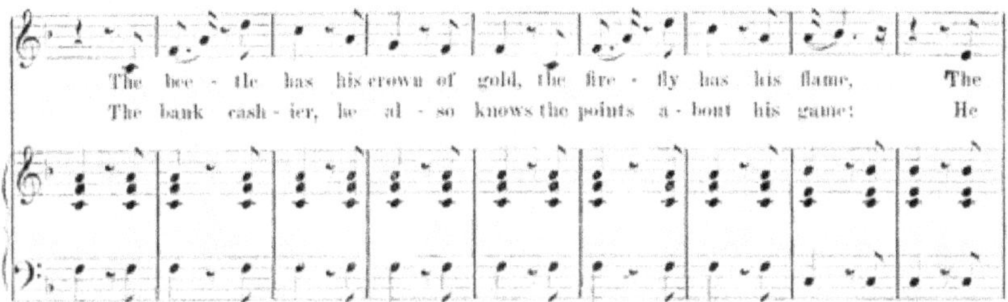
The bee - tle has his crown of gold, the fire - fly has his flame, The
The bank cash - ier, he al - so knows the points a - bout his game: He

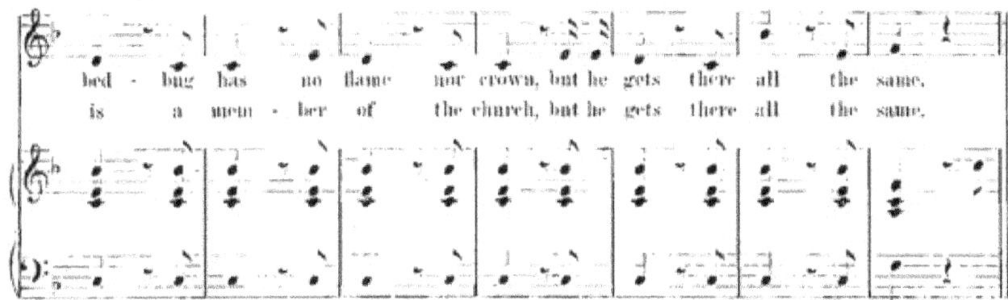
bed - bug has no flame nor crown, but he gets there all the same.
is a mem - ber of the church, but he gets there all the same.

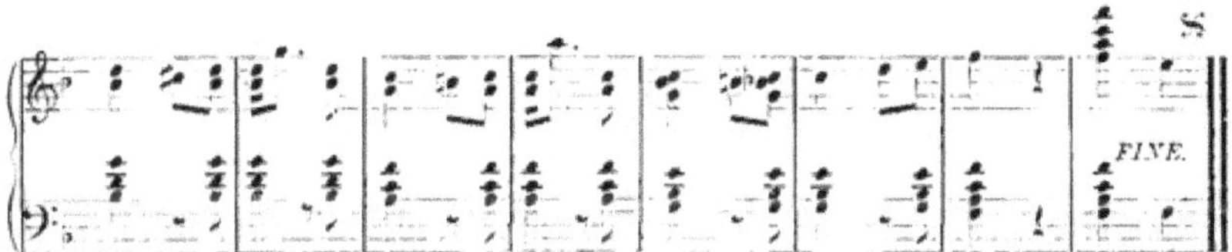
FINE.

3. The millionaire has money bags, and many bonds and stocks,
He owns a railroad, too, and has substantial bus'ness blocks;
But when the winter days have come, with cold we all exclaim.
The plumber has no stocks or bonds, but he gets there just the same.

4. The game of poker I enjoy, of it I never tire.
To sit behind four aces is a thing I much admire,
But when with aces four I sit, and think I'll scoop the game,
A little straight flush don't look big, but it gets there all the same.

5. Tho' many fall by fire and sword, and yield up their last breaths,
The perils of the railroad, too, cause many sudden deaths.
In deadly mines beneath the earth fire-damp doth kill or maim.
Toy-pistols don't amount to much, but they get there just the same.

6. The roller skate has often caused a dull and sick-'ning thud,
While others fall a victim to the thick and slip-p'ry mud.
But when it comes to shaking up a person's mortal frame,
The innocent banana peel will get there all the same.

HOW IS YOUR SISTER MARY.

Words and Music by **BILLY ROBINSON.**

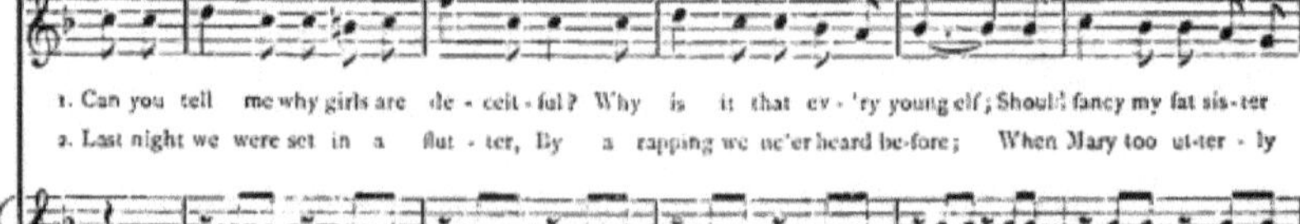

1. Can you tell me why girls are de - ceit - ful? Why is it that ev - 'ry young elf; Should fancy my fat sis - ter
2. Last night we were set in a flut - ter, By a rapping we ne'er heard be-fore; When Mary too ut-ter - ly

Ma - ry, And al - low me to fan - cy my - self, Should I meet with Tom, Dick or Har - ry, No mat - ter
ut - ter, To ans - wer the knock at the door; I flew through the hall in a hur - ry, Queer-no-tions

how press-ing the task They'll man-age a mo-ment to tar - ry, And this is the ques-tion they'll ask,
were fill - ing my head; I o-pened the door in a flur - ry, When a dude young fel-low he said:

CHORUS.

How is your sis - ter Ma - ry? I hope her health is fair; How is her pet can-
How is your sis - ter Ma - ry? I hope her health is fair; How is her pet can-

a - ry? Does she still bang her hair? The ques - tion nev - er va - ry, We
a - ry? Does she still bang her hair? The ques - tion nev - er va - ry, We
hear it ev - 'ry where; How is your sis - ter Ma - ry? Does she still bang her hair?
hear it ev - 'ry where; How is your sis - ter Ma - ry? Does she still bang her hair?
Repeat 8va.
D.C.

BLACK-EYED BESSIE LYLE.

Revised and arr. by C. L. KECK. Music by T. R. WALKER.

INTRODUCTION.
Andante con espress.

8va

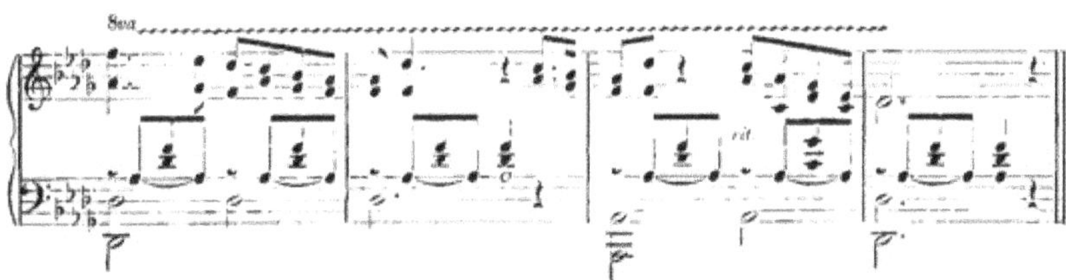
8va
rit

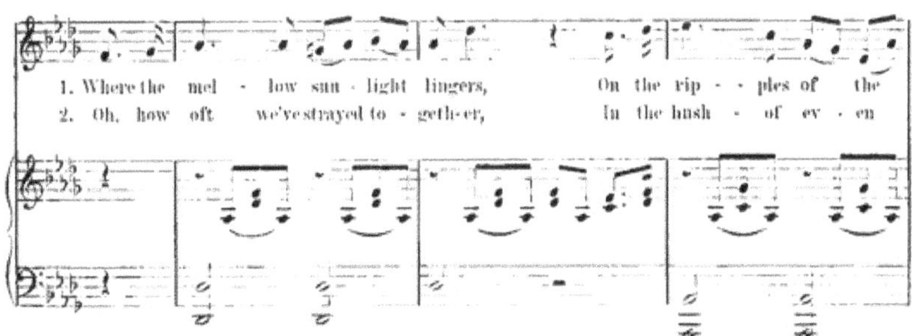
1. Where the mel - low sun - light lingers, On the rip - - ples of the
2. Oh, how oft we've strayed to - geth - er, In the hush - of ev - en

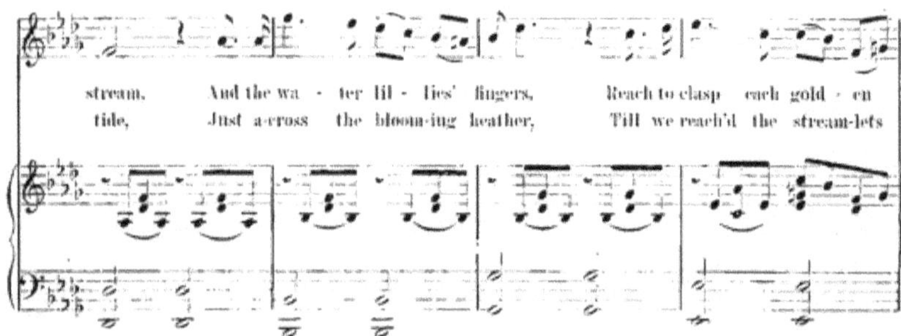
stream, And the wa - ter lil - lies' fingers, Reach to clasp each gold - en
tide, Just a-cross the bloom-ing heather, Till we reach'd the stream-lets

gleam; Close be-side the mur-m'ring waters, Mir-ror'd in the sun - beams
side; While the twi - light shed its glo-ries, And the stars of heav - en

smile, Watch-ing, wait-ing, some one loi-ters— 'Tis my black-eyed Bes-sie Lyle.
smile'd, There I whis-per'd sweet-est stor ies, To my black eyed Bes-sie Lyle.

CHORUS.

Black eyed Bes - sie, how I love her, With a heart so free from
Black eyed Bes-sie how I love her, With a heart so free from

rit.
guile. Tru-er than the stars a - bove her, Is my Black eyed Bes - sie Lyle.
rit.
guile. True-r than the stars a-bove her, Is my black eyed Bes-sie Lyle.
ritard.

The Chinese, The Chinese, You Know!

JOHN E. DONNELLY.
Moderato.
INTRO.
f
VOICE.
1. I'll sing of a sub - ject, but your ears you must lend; And lis - ten to what I've to say.............. We'll have to do something with this curse in our
2. Large meet - ings were held, and loud speech - es were made, By men who had ax - es to grind........... They spoke of our cause and they prom - ised us
3. Now what shall we do with our girls and our boys? Is a quest - ion that we must decide.......... If they don't learn to toil, why they sure - ly will

Three plates.

land, For our bois - ness has gone to de - cay......... The merchants are id - le their
laws, But a - las! it was all for a blind...... They know what we need But our
spoil, And so - ci - ety will cast them a - side..... They will wan - der for - lorn with
goods on their hands, And the cause of this ter - ri - ble woe......... I'll tell you my
cries they won't heed, In con - gress they work ver - y slow......... And they are still
the finger of scorn, Point-ing at them where - ev - er they go........... And they will fill
friends and you'll say I am right, It's the chin - ese, the chin - ese, you know..........
coming here yes, ten-thousand a year, The chin - ese, the chin - ese, you know..........
early graves through these mongolian slaves, The chin - ese, the chin - ese, you know..........

CHORUS.
Let la - bor and cap - i - tal, go hand in hand; And crush out this

ter - ri - ble for............ For a cry - ing disgrace, is this a - bom - in - a - ble

D.C. to 𝄋
race, The chin - ese, the chin - ese, you know..................

ELSIE DARLING I AM WAITING.

Words by CHAS. H. DOUTRICK. Music by JNO. S. COX.

INTRODUCTION.
Allegro moderato.
mf
1. The flow'rs are droop - ing in the dew, Of eve - ning El sie dear........... As
2. Sweet is the eve - ning darl - ing one, The moon will soon come forth,........ To
3. We'll sit be - side the riv - er, where The wa - ter lil - ies grow,.......... And
piu.

by the gate I stand and wait. For your fond smile of cheer.......... The
smile up - on us— she you know, All lov - ers scenes do court;.......... And
ex - change words of hope - ful love, With naught to check the flow;.......... And
birds have ceased their song of joy. The sky's no long - er blue.......... And
as we'll stroll up - on the green. Our troths we'll plight a - new.......... It
of that hap - py day we'll talk, When no longer we'll be two.......... Oh
by the gate I watch and wait. Sweet El - sie dear for you..........
gives me joy sweet El - sie love, To watch and wait for you..........
dar - ling El - sie, pa - tient - ly;— I wait and watch for you..........

CHORUS.
SOPRANO.
El - sie dar - ling I am wait - ing, For you so dear and true,...... My
ALTO.
TENOR.
El - sie dar - ling I am wait - ing, For you so dear and true,...... My......
BASS.
heart is beat - ing joy - ous, While wait - ing here for you............
heart is beat - ing joy - ous, While wait - ing here for you............

DANDY SERVANTS.

By G. B. BRIGHAM.

INTRODUCTION.

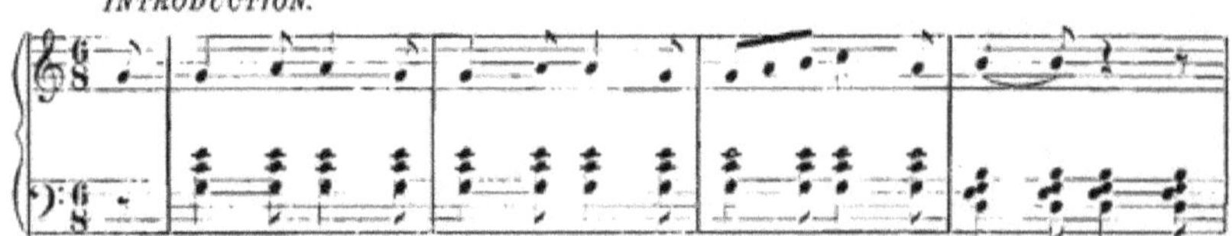

1. We
2. We're

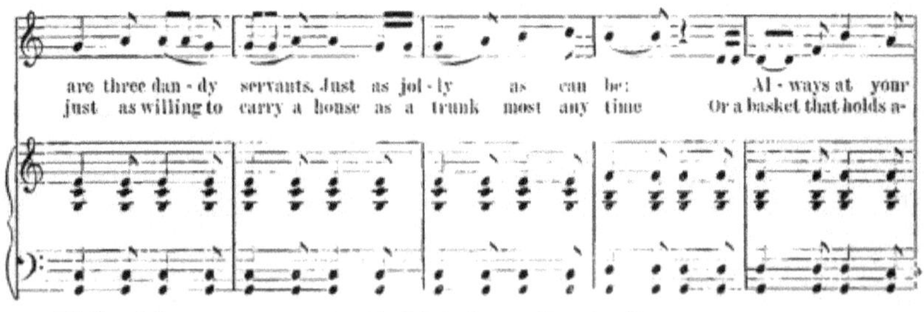
are three dan - dy servants. Just as jol - ly as can be: Al - ways at your
just as willing to carry a house as a trunk most any time Or a basket that holds a-

ser - vice and a hap - py lot are we Running here and running there We
bout a ton.... all for a nickle or dime. Some-times we have to drive a span. We

go where e'er we please, Coaches and bunks, va - lises and trunks We car-ry at our ease. Then
don't mind that you know, But do it ver - y grace - ful - ly As on our way we go.

Chorus.
Heigh! heigh! ho! on we go, Mer-ri ly on our way...... With a hip! ha! la! and

Ha! ha! ha! hap-pi-ly ev - 'ry day....... We mind our mas-ters to a dot, and

never ob - jec - tion see......... You'll al - ways find us happy and gay, For dan - dy servants are

we, are we, You'll al - ways find us happy and gay. For dandy ser-vants are we.
8va

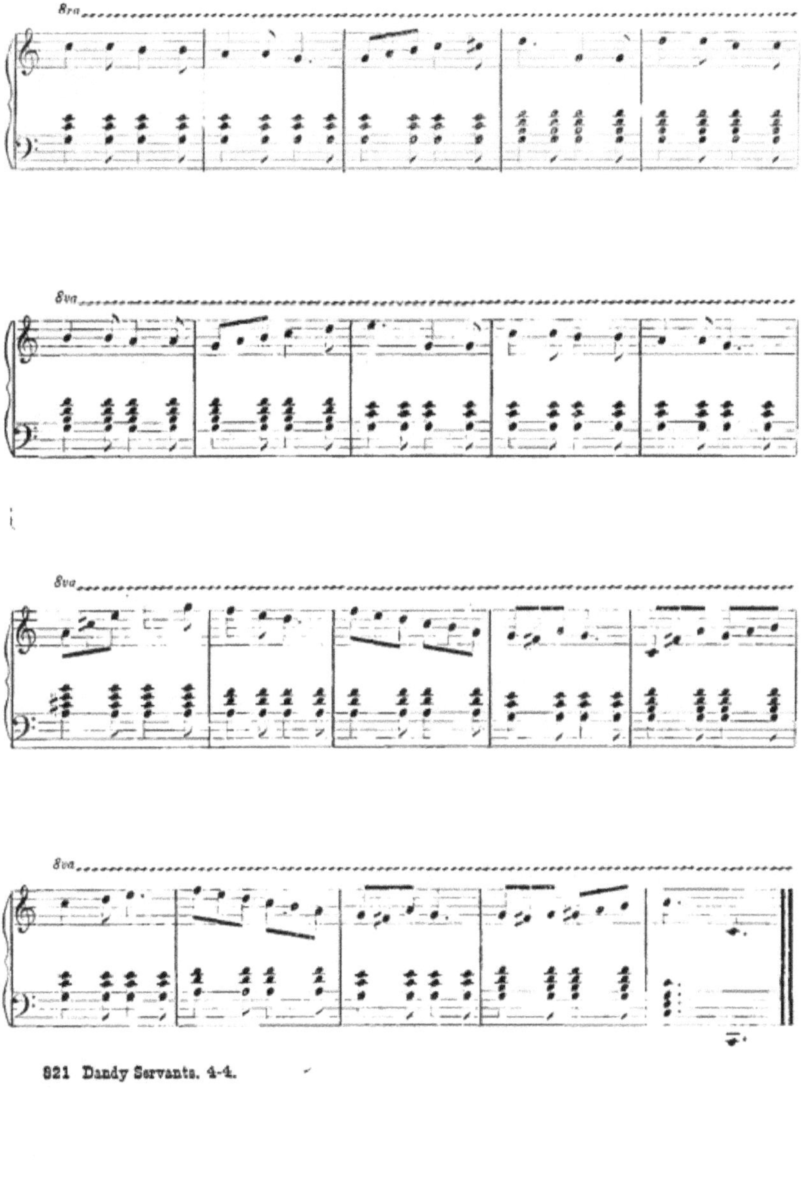

8va

8va

8va

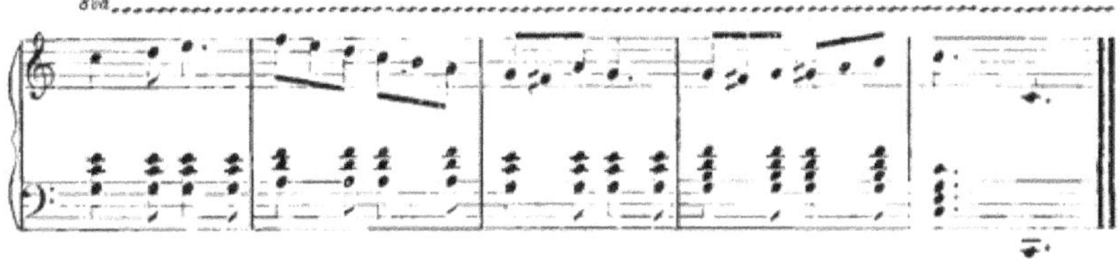
8va

821 Dandy Servants. 4-4.

JANIE.

Words by HELEN WHITNEY CLARKE.

Music by T. R. WALKER.
Revised and arr. by C. L. KECK.

Introduction.
Moderato
mf
p
1. The dai - sy held her dain - ty cup, To catch the dew-drops bright, The
2. The swal-lows flit - ted here and there, The bat had left his bow'r, The
bee had kiss'd the clo - ver - bobs, And bade them all good-night; The
prim - rose, with a bash - ful air, Un - clos'd her pet - al'd flow'r; The
Ka - ty - did had tuned her song, A - mong the ap - ple boughs, And
Whip - poor - will his plain - tive tale, Pro-claim'd 'neath wood - ed boughs, And

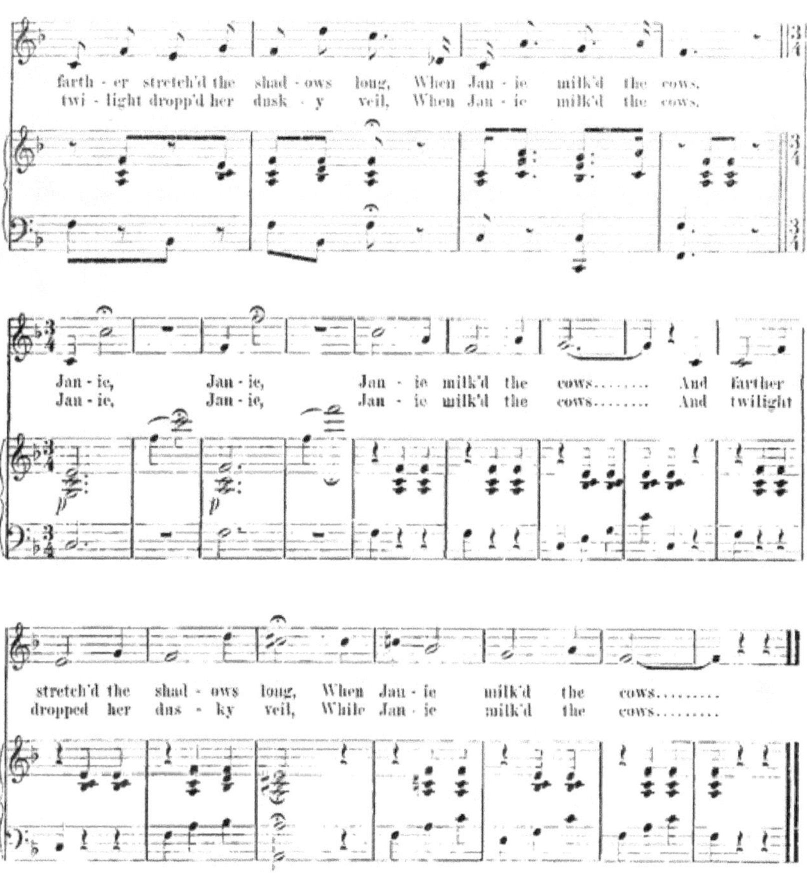
farth - er stretch'd the shad - ows long, When Jan - ie milk'd the cows.
twi - light dropp'd her dusk - y veil, When Jan - ie milk'd the cows.
Jan - ie, Jan - ie, Jan - ie milk'd the cows........ And farther
Jan - ie, Jan - ie, Jan - ie milk'd the cows........ And twilight
stretch'd the shad - ows long, When Jan - ie milk'd the cows.........
dropped her dus - ky veil, While Jan - ie milk'd the cows.........

3.

And Ben, the plow boy, strolling by
Comes thro' the open bars,
While softly in the Western sky.
Shine out the tranquil stars,
And while the corn blades whisper low,
Two lovers pledge their vows,
Amid the twilight's purple glow,
Where Janie milked the cows.

4.

A little cottage, snug and new.
With hop-vines at the door.
The Sunbeams peeping softly through,
Lie dancing on the floor.
And when the first pale evening stars
Shine thro the forest boughs.
Young farmer Ben, beside the bars,
Helps Janie milk the cows.

Respectfully Inscribed to Mrs. WILLIAM WIRT SMITH.

Dear Love, a Sweet Good-night.

C. L. JENKS, Jr.

INTRODUCTION.
Andantino.

f
p
pp

p
cres.
dim.
Where fall the twi - light shad - ows, Seek-ing for thee, Oh
And, when in peace - ful slum - ber Dreaming, to thee I'd
p

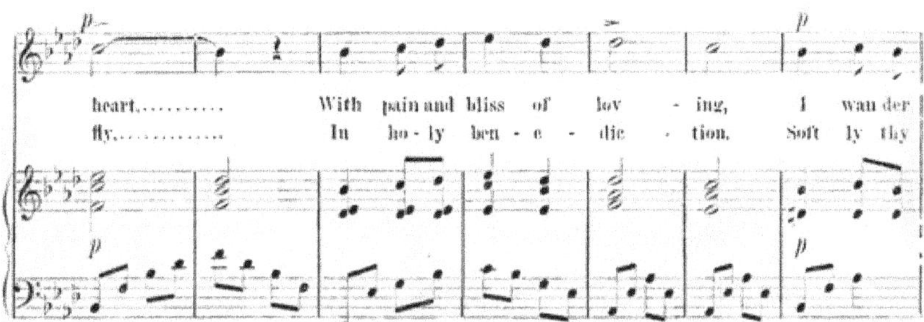
heart.......... With pain and bliss of lov - ing, I wan-der
fly............ In ho - ly ben - e - dic - tion. Soft - ly thy

cres.
where thou art;....... From out my soul in si - - lence,
name I'd sigh;...... Then swift on air - y pin - ions,

cres - - cen - - do.
Up - well - ing pure... and bright,......... I send a thou - sand
A bird-ling speeds its flight,......... And light - ly hov - 'ring

ff
rit e dim.
p
FINE.
greet - ings. Dear love, a sweet good night........
o'er................ thee. Sings in thy heart "Good night."......
ff
p
FINE

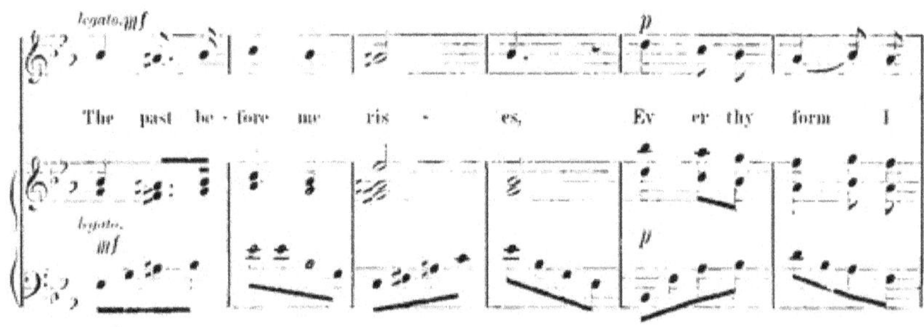
legato. mf
The past be - fore me ris - es, Ev - er thy form I
p
legato.
mf
p

see:.............. A spir - it soft - ly glid - ing.

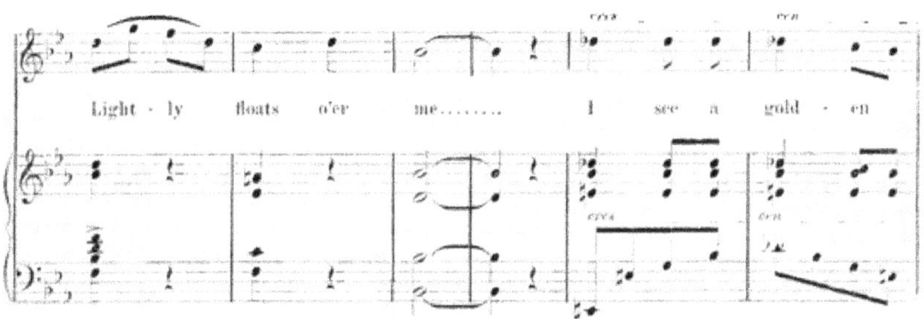
cres
cen
Light - ly floats o'er me........ I see a gold - en
cres
cen

do.
f
morn - ing, When joy my heart... will fill;......... A flood of
do.
f

p
D. S.
sweet e mo - tion.... My ten der bos - om thrill.....
p
D. S.

DEY STOLE MY CHILD AWAY.

("THE VIRGINIA ROSE BUD.")

Composed and sung by F. H. Kavanaugh.

Allegretto.
f
p
1. I had a rose - bud in my gar-den growing,...A plant I cher - ished with a father's
2. Oh,then this heart was withered and de - ject-ed....I wandered thro' the fields,but all in
care,When oth - er dar-kies round that plant was hoeing.Its zef - fer-es-sence seemed to fill the
vain, And ev - 'ry plant on me a shade reflected...The tears they fell a - round me like the
air; Oh, how I watched that little plant while creeping.She,like her moth-er, always light and
rain; The sun a - bove looked down upon my sorrow. My heart was wither'd,I sought for her in

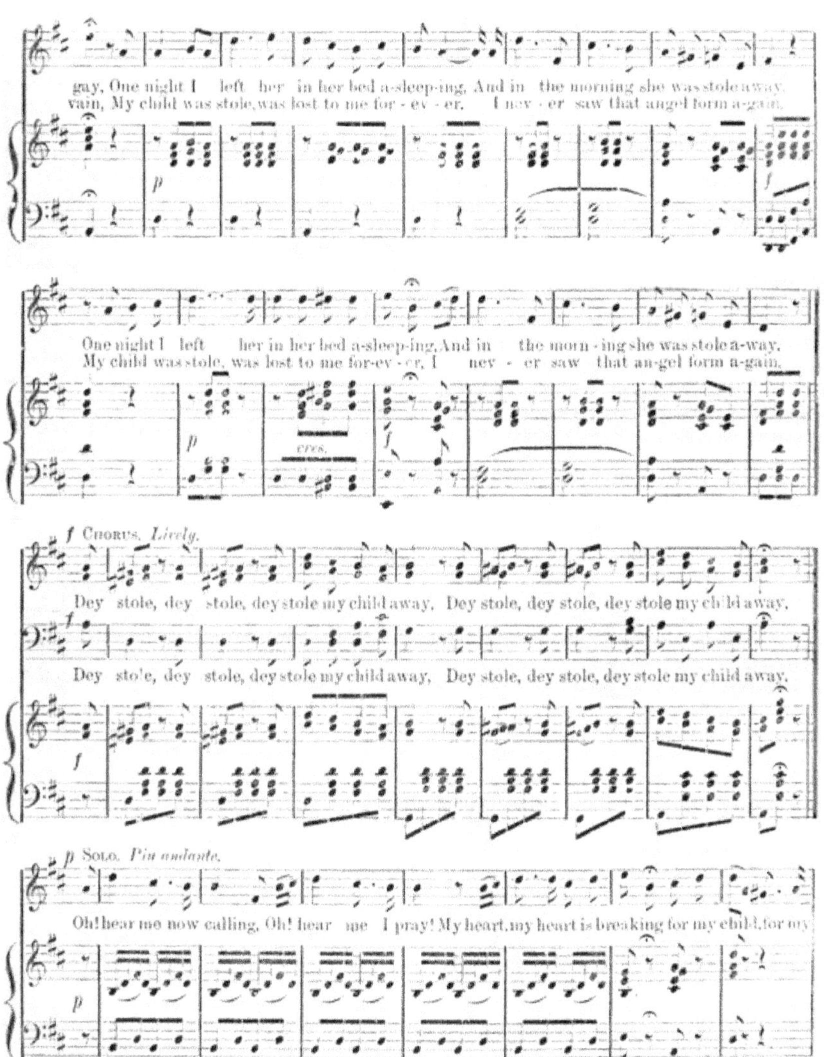
gay, One night I left her in her bed a-sleep-ing, And in the morning she was stole away,
vain, My child was stole, was lost to me for - ev - er, I nev - er saw that angel form a-gain,
p
f
One night I left her in her bed a-sleep-ing, And in the morn - ing she was stole a-way,
My child was stole, was lost to me for-ev - er, I nev - er saw that an-gel form a-gain,
p
cres.
f
f Chorus. Lively.
Dey stole, dey stole, dey stole my child away, Dey stole, dey stole, dey stole my child away,
f
Dey sto!e, dey stole, dey stole my child away, Dey stole, dey stole, dey stole my child away,
f
p Solo. Più andante.
Oh! hear me now calling, Oh! hear me I pray! My heart, my heart is breaking for my child, for my
p

Ad lib.
Chorus.
Solo.
Chorus.
child dey stole a - way. Oh! oh! oh! hear dat voice! Oh! oh! oh! hear dat voice!
hear dat voice! hear dat voice!
f Chorus. Allegro.
I hear dar hoofs op-on de hill, I hear dem faint - er, faint - er still, I hear dar hoofs op-
I hear dar hoofs op-on de hill, I hear dem faint - er, faint - er still, I hear dar hoofs op-
on de hill, I hear dem faint-er, faint-er still. Dey stole, dey stole,.. dey
on de hill, I hear dem faint-er, faint-er still, Dey stole, dey stole,.. dey

stole my child a - way, Dey stole, dey stole, dey stole my child a - way, my
stole my child a - way, Dey stole, dey stole, dey stole my child a - way, my
8va
child a - way, my child a - way, my child a - - - way.
child a - way, my child a - way, my child a - - - way,
dim.

YES, I'LL BE DAR.

Composed by JACOB J. SAWYER.

ALLEGRO.

Moderato.
When I was down in E - gypt land, Tell dem I will be.... dar; I....
As I was cross - ing yon - der field, Tell dem I will be.... dar; I....

took my breth - ren by de hand and told him I'd be dar. Oh,
had my breast - plate, sword and shield, tell dem I'll be dar. Oh, de

shout, you chil - dren, shout, you free! Tell dem I will be dar too; For....
gates am gold and de hin - ges, too, Tell dem I will be dar too; And....
be has bo't your lib - er - ty, So tell them I'll be dar, yes, I'll
dey are free for me and you, So tell them I'll be dar, yes, I'll
CHORUS.
be dar, I'll be dar, Bright and ear - ly in de morn - ing, child, I'll be dar, I'll
be dar, I'll be dar, Bright and ear - ly in de morn - ing, child, I'll be dar, I'll

be dar, be - fore de broke of day; Oh, yes, I'll be dar, I'll be dar, Right
be dar, be - fore de broke of day; Oh, yes, I'll be dar, I'll be dar, Right
ear - ly in de morn - ing, child, I'll be dar, I'll be dar, be - fore de broke of day.
ear - ly in de morn - ing, child, I'll be dar, I'll be dar, be - fore de broke of day.

I'll be dar.

LILLIAN, I WAIT FOR THEE.

SONG.

Words and Music by G. B. BRIGHAM.

INTRODUCTION. *Andante.*

Affetuoso.

1. Lil - lian, Loved one, I am wait - ing. When you're far from
2. Lil - lian, Loved one, don't for - get me: While you're far a -

me............... How se - rene and calm the mo - ments,
way.............. Just re - mem - ber me in kind - ness.

Amoroso.
While I a-wait for thee..............
Think of me ev - ry day.............
Hea - ven with its rays of
Let the an-gels guard thy

sun - shine Bright - ens up my heart...........
slum - ber While you sleep at night...........

Then all is sad un - til to - mor row. while we're thus..... a
And at day be joy - ous ev - er. May your cares be always

part,..............
light..............
Lil - lian, Loved one, I am wait - ing.
Lil - lian. Loved one, while you leave me;

When you're far from me..............
You are ev - er near,..............
All my dreams are
For you leave a

of you, loved one, Lil - lian I wait for thee..............
heart in sad - ness. Lil - lian I wait for thee..............

A TRIP TO THE COUNTRY.

Words by CLARK WISE. Music by A. MANN.

Introduction
mf
1. I took a trip to the coun - try, To vis - it my moth'r-in - law, And
2. Lit - tle but - ter - flies made but - ter, The bum - ble bees were busy too, And
3. Oh! you could see the lit - tle pigs, Climbing up the trees so high, And
if you will kind - ly lis - ten, I'll tell you what I saw, The
the gob - bler seem'd of - fi - cious, Shout - ing his "Peek - a - boo," The
sing in most mel - o - dious tones; "Wait till the clouds roll by," In

Two plates.

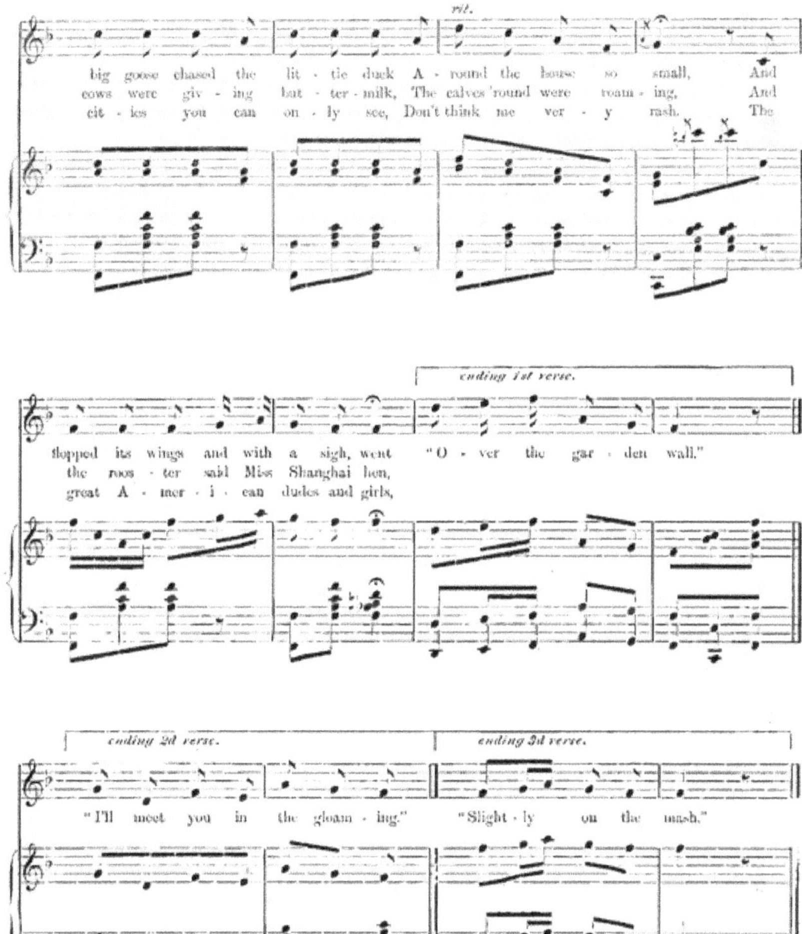
rit.
big goose chased the lit - tle duck A - round the house so small, And
cows were giv - ing but - ter - milk, The calves 'round were roam - ing, And
cit - ies you can on - ly see, Don't think me ver - y rash. The
flopped its wings and with a sigh, went
the roos - ter said Miss Shanghai hen,
great A - mer - i - can dudes and girls,
ending 1st verse.
"O - ver the gar - den wall."
ending 2d verse.
"I'll meet you in the gloam - ing."
ending 3d verse.
"Slight - ly on the mash."

"Hurrah! for Co. B."

Words and Music by Gus B. Brigham.

INTRODUCTION. La Militaire.

1. I'll
2. O!
3. A

sing of an or-gan-i-za tion, that you will of-ten meet, . . . With
watch the time, aint it fine! they're drilled down to a "T." . . . .
jol-li-er crowd of boys in line, . . . Nev-er can be found. . . .

ban - ners high, as they go by, a march - ing up the street; . . . . With
Ev' - ry one ad - mires them, where - ev - er they may be; . . . . . . And
"Right dress, Company front!" you see they don't look round; . . . . With
u - ni - forms so gay and fine, you'll hear the peo - ple say, ... When
when they're on the line of march they al - ways lead the way, ... And
mus - kets bright, and step so light, they brave - ly march a - way; . . . . . The
stand - ing by, they all will cry, . . . "B" is out to - day, ...
all the high - toned peo - ple cry, . . . "B" is out to - day, ... "A -
First Bri - gade are to the front, "B" is out to - day, ...

Here they come, in "sin - gle file," just watch their mo - tions new;
- bout face! guide right!" the Cap - tain gives com - mand.
"Form pla - toons! fours right!" they quick - ly move a - bout.
Now in "twos" they change a - bout, the lines are pass - ing through,
"Left wheel! coun - ter - march!" you will see it's grand.
"Dou - ble rank to rear march!" the Cap - tain he will shout.
In - to "fours" they're marching by, the band be - gins to play, ... Hur -
"Col - umn left! Forward all!" they march in time a - way. . . . . . Hur -
"Left o - blique! Aim! fire!" no word have they to say. . . . . . Hur -
- rah, hur - rah! for "Com-pa - ny B. they're on pa - rade to - day! . . . .
Hurrah! for Co. B. 5.

CHORUS.
"Forward march! Shoulder arms!" while marching up the street, "Fours right! Company halt!" you
bet they can't be beat! "Present arms! salute again!" on drill you all can see, They
march a - bout, and the peo - ple shout, "Hur-rah for Company B!"
1
2

3

THE VILLAGE PEDDLER.

SONG FOR BARITONE.

Words by EUSTACE.
G. GARIBOLDI.
Allegretto vivace.
Ah!
a tempo.
1 I wend my way so mer - ry, My bur-den fair I car - ry; Come la - dies fair nor tar - ry! "Come buy of me," I cry, Don't scorn me, dame nor maid - en! With joys for you I'm la - den, The vil-lage ped-dler I! the vil-lage ped - dler am I!
2 I've rib - bons for your fac - es, And neat and pret-ty lac - es To give you airs and grac - es That make the men to sigh! Ring - lets of gold - en brightness, And gloves of dain - ty white - ness, The vil-lage ped-dler I! the vil-lage ped - dler am I!
3 For cheeks grown pale, I've ros - es, I've pow-der for red nos - es! I've kiss - es sweet as pos - ies For lips would like to try! Then come each dame and maid - en! With joys my pack is la - den, The vil-lage ped-dler I! the vil-lage ped - dler am I!
Tra
cres.
col canto.
dim.

4
la! Tra la! The vil-lage ped-dler I! 1 & 2, Tra la, tra la, Who'll buy, who'll buy? Tra
3. Come, girls, and deck your-selves with care. If
cres.
p staccato.
la, tra la! Who'll buy, who'll buy? Tra la, tra la, who'll buy, who'll buy? the vil-lage ped-dler
you some gen-tle swain would snare! There's none so old that need de-spair, the vil-lage ped-dler
cres.
1st and 2d time.
I!
I!
ff
pesante.
D.S.
3d time
2 I've I! Tra la la la la! Tra la la la
3 For
D.S.

la! Tra la la ra la la ra la la ra la la ra la la la, tra la la la la, The
Presto.
p
rinculendosi.
Ped.
vil-lage ped-dler I! Tra la la ra la la ra la la ra la la ra la la la, tra la la la la! The
Presto.
Ped.
vil-lage ped-dler I! Tra la la la la! tra la la la la, la la la
p
f
ff
la la la la la la la la la la la la!
Ped.

LITTLE SWEETHEART, SAY GOOD BYE.

Words and Music by **JACOB J. SAWER.**

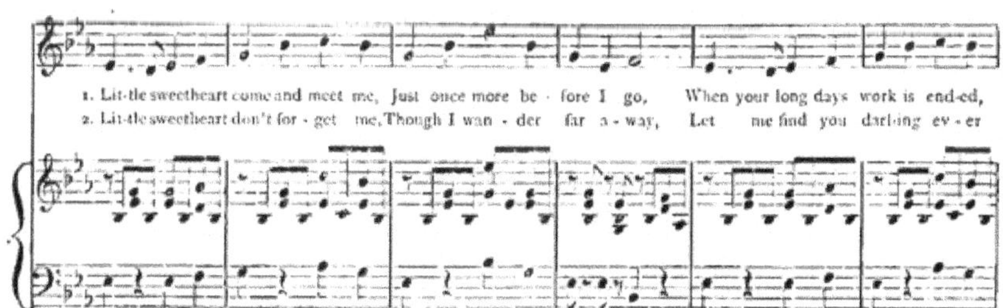
1. Lit-tle sweetheart come and meet me, Just once more be - fore I go, When your long days work is end-ed,
2. Lit-tle sweetheart don't for - get me, Though I wan - der far a - way, Let me find you darl-ing ev - er

when the sun is sink ing low; Let us wan - der once to - geth - er, down the old rose bor - der'd lane,
as I leave you now to - day; Let me find what ere may hap-pen, let me find when ere I come,
Who can tell what change may wait us, ere we two shall meet a - gain, For I know what ere may hap-pen,
Still my lit - tle sweet-heart read - y with her lov - ing wel-come home, Come what will I'll still re-mem-ber,
Lit - tle sweet-heart, you will be through all change of time or for-tune, Just as dear and true to me.
How we've been just you and I, all the world to one an - oth - er, Lit - tle sweet-heart, say good-by.

CHORUS.

Soprano.
Lit - tle sweet - heart, look up smil - ing, As you smiled in years gone by,
Alto.
Tenor.
Lit - tle sweet - heart, look up smil - ing, As you smiled in years gone by,
Bass.
ff
p
pp
Brave - ly with a whis - per'd bless - ing, Lit - tle sweet - heart, say good - by.
ff
p
pp
Brave - ly with a whis - per'd bless - ing, Lit - tle sweet - heart, say good - by.
ff
p
pp

HE WAS A CARELESS MAN.

GEO. GOLDSMITH Jr.

PIANO.
p
f
p ad lib.
sf Allegretto.
sf
1. There was a man whose care - less - ness ob - tained for him a name, He
2. To pass as a phil - an - thro - pist, it was his con - stant aim, And
3. His gen - er - os - i - ty was tho't to be his no - blest gift, He'd
ne - ver look'd at trades - men's bills, or ques - tion'd an - y claim, He
no sub - scrip - tion list ap - pear'd with - out his no - ble name; Com -
call a han - som cab to give a weal thy aunt a lift, Al -
thought that time was made for slaves, He griev'd when folks were vex'd, And
pared with his do - na - tion, ev' - ry oth - er seem'd a speck, But
though it was a fact, of which he then was un - a - ware, He

CHORUS.
nev - er did a thing to - day, that could be done the next.
pure - ly thro' for - get - ful - ness, He nev - er sent his cheque.
al - ways got out first, and left his aunt to pay the fare.
He was a care - less man, He

was a care - less man, It troubled him much to think, he was such a ver - y care - less man.

4. His friends he very often asked to dinner, ball, or rout,
   They hoped to find him *in*, of course, but always found him ***out***;
He went to Margate last July and met with much reverse,
   His friends there had to keep him, he forgot to take his purse. Cho.

5. He took a *third* class ticket on the railway, but alas!
   He was so very negligent, he travelled by *first* class;
He always had refreshment till he heard the station bell,
   And when the train was moving off, he hurried off as well. Cho.

6. He rarely lived in one place long, his nature was to roam,
   And when the gas and poor-rates called, he never was at home;
He well insured his furniture, a caution wisely learnt,
   But rashly spilt some paraffin, and ev'ry stick was burnt. Cho.

7. Whene'er he went to any kind of party, I am told,
   He always wore an overcoat, not only cheap, but old,
He hung it in the hall, and when he bade the host adieu,
   He went off in some-one-else's coat, that happened to be new. Cho.

When E'er I See Those Smiling Eyes.

DUET AND CHORUS.

Words by THOMAS MOORE. Music by D. H. MAGILL.

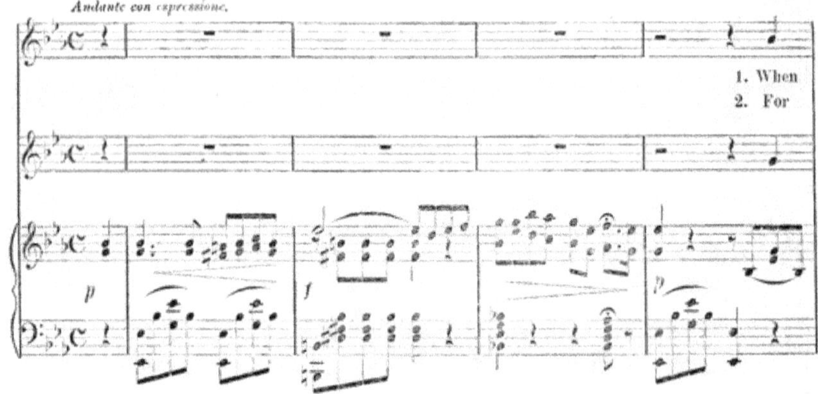
Andante con espressione.
1. When
2. For
p
f
p

e'er I see those smil-ing eyes, All filled with hope, and joy, and light, As if no
time will come with all its blights, The ru - ined hope, the friend unkind, The love that

cloud could ev - - er rise, ... To dim a heav'n so pure - ly
leaves, where e'er it lights, ... A chilled or burn - ing heart be
bright, I sigh to think how soon that brow, ... In
hind, While youth that now like snow ap - pears, ... E're
grief may lose its ev - 'ry ray, And that light heart so joy - ous
sul - lied by the darkening rain, When once 'tis touched by sor - row's

ad lib.
now, ... Al - most for - get it once was gay.
tears, ... Will nev - er shine so bright a - gain.

Chorus.
Soprano.
Those smil - ing eyes, All filled with light, As if no
Alto.
Tenor.
Those smil-ing eyes, All filled with light,
Bass.
Piano.

cloud could ev - er rise, As if no cloud could ev - er, ev - er
As is no cloud could ev - er rise, cloud could ev - er, ev - er

rise, . . . To dim a heav'n so pure - ly bright.
rise . . . To dim a heav'n so pure - ly bright.

RING DEM CHIMIN' BELLS.

JACOB J. SAWYER.

1st.
2d.
1. Go tell old Pomp and Hannah Brown To ring dem chim-in' bells, Yes, tell dem all for
2. De streets up dar am paved wid gold, Ring dem chim-in' bells, And dar we am not
miles around To ring dem chim-in' bells; Dis am de day of ju - bi - lee,
bo't and sold, So ring dem chim-in' bells; De children dar am robed in white,
Ring dem chim-in' bells, 'Kase Mas-sa Linkum sot us free, So ring dem chim-in' bells. Yes,
Ring dem chim-in' bells, De black man dar's as good as white, So ring dem chim-in' bells. Yes,

CHORUS.
Hal - le - lu - jah! shout and sing,... Won't we make de heav - ens ring,....
Hal - le - lu - jah! shout and sing,... Won't we make de heav - ens ring,....
When de chil - dren chant and sing,... Den you'll hear dem ole bells ring.
When de chil - dren chant and sing,... Den you'll hear dem ole bells ring.

To my friend, BILLY [illegible]

JERUSALEM ROAD.

By DAN LEWIS.

Moderato.
Introduction.
1. The chariots getting ready, and I must go Off on Je-ru-sa-lem road, I'll
2. Stand back dear brothers, don't you get in my way, Off on Je-ru-sa-lem road,

Three pages.

pack up mighty quick, and I wont be slow, Off on Je - ru - sa - lem road, There's no
like you mighty well, but I can - not stay, Off on Je - ru - sa - lem road, So tell
f
p

cars or boat or rivers that's wide, Off on Je - ru - sa - lem road, If you
all the peo - ple that I'm gwine, Off on Je - ru - sa - lem road, If they
f
p

catch the chariot you can ride, Off on Je - ru - sa - lem road.
get the grace they'll come a - long, Off on Je - ru - sa - lem road.
f

CHORUS.
I'm a gwine - ing, yes, I'm a gwine - ing, Deed, I'm a gwine - ing,
Off on Je - ru - sa - lem road,
I'm a gwine - ing,
yes, I'm a gwine - ing, Deed, I'm a gwine - ing, Off on Je - ru - sa - lem road.

3. I done my best for to stay with you, I must
Go on Jerusalem road,
So this is my chance and I'm going right through.
Off on the Jerusalem road.
The devil's mighty cunning, which everybody knows, I must
Go on Jerusalem road,
If you aint got the grace, he'll catch you sure, so
Come on Jerusalem road.

Chorus, and repeat.

Where the Morning Glories Twine.

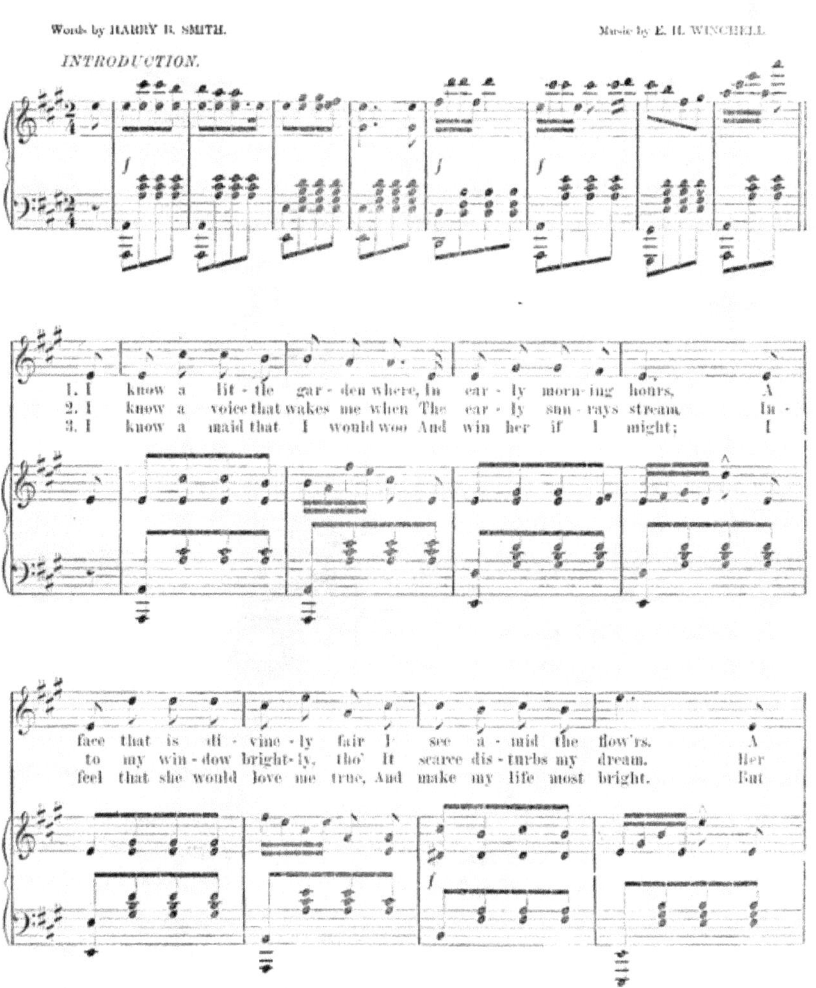
Words by HARRY B. SMITH.
Music by E. H. WINCHELL.
INTRODUCTION.
1. I know a lit - tle gar - den where, In ear - ly morn - ing hours, A
2. I know a voice that wakes me when The ear - ly sun - rays stream, In -
3. I know a maid that I would woo And win her if I might; I
face that is di - vine - ly fair I see a - mid the flow'rs. A
to my win - dow bright - ly, tho' It scarce dis - turbs my dream. Her
feel that she would love me true, And make my life most bright. But

face that like a pic - ture bright, Is framed a - mid the vine. A -
laugh is light, her song is sweet 'Tis to my win - dow borne. By
still I dare not speak of love, How ev - er hard I strive. For
bout her lat - tice win - dow, Where the morn - ing glo - ries twine.
sum - mer zeph - yrs wing - ing, Like a greet - ing in the morn.
I'm a man of thir - ty, She a lit - tle miss of five.
REFRAIN.
And bright - er there the sun light beams, Than on the gar - den gay. To
love her face the sun light seems, And love her well it may. A
f
f

face half hid in flow'rs a - mid The Hon - ey Suck - le vine. Each
morn she's at her lat - tice, Where the morn - ing glo - ries twine.
INTERLUDE. Dance ad lib.

The Songs that Mother Sung.

TENOR SOLO, WITH QUARTETTE FOR MALE VOICES.

S. F. COMPTON.

TENOR.
dolce
1 I hear the songs they sing to-day, But nev - er one is sweet As those my moth-er sang to me When sit - ting at her feet. My thoughts go back to childhood years, When hope and I were young, And as of old I hear to-day The songs my moth - er sung.
2 At twi - light's hour I of - ten dream I am a child once more; I seek the house where I was born, I pass the o - pen door. There moth - er rocks be-side the hearth, Her lit - tle ones a - mong, And life for-gets its cares to hear The songs my moth - er sung.
3 O, long the grass has grown a - bove That lov - ing moth - er's face, But still in faithful hearts she keeps Her old, her dear old place. No oth - er songs can be so sweet As those we heard when young, When sit - ting at our moth-er's knee— The songs my moth - er sung.
rit.
a tempo.

QUARTETTE.
1st TENOR.
The songs my moth - er sung The songs my moth - er sung, And
The songs my moth - er sung The songs my moth - er sung, And
The songs my moth - er sung The songs my moth - er sung, When
2d TENOR.
1st BASS.
The songs my moth - er sung, The songs my moth - er sung, And
The songs my moth - er sung, The songs my moth - er sung, And
The songs my moth - er sung, The songs my moth - er sung, When
2d BASS.
Rit.
as of old I hear to - day The songs my moth - er sung.
life for - gets its cares to hear The songs my moth - er sung.
sit - ting at our moth-er's knee— The songs my moth - er sung.
rit.
as of old I hear to - day The songs my moth - er sung.
life for - gets its cares to hear The songs my moth - er sung.
sit - ting at our moth-er's knee— The songs my moth - er sung.
rit.

612. The Songs that Mother Sung. 2-2.

Girl on the Rolling Skates.

ARR. L. VON DER MEHDEN.
Words and Music by DAN LEWIS.
Tempo di Schottische.
mf
1st.
2d.
Tempo di Valse.
1. I'll tell you of a beau-ty I met the oth - er day.......... When
2. I real - ly love en - joy - ment, In such a pleas - ant way.......... On
3. By - ci - cle that is pleas - ant, Some peo - ple say 'tis nice.......... Or
first my eyes be-held her, I was complete - ly carried a - way.......... She was
such a great improvement, The top - - ic of the day.......... Boat
e - ven in the Win-ter, The skat - ing on the ice.......... I

such a lit - tle an - gel, I nev - er can for - get.............. And
sail - ing that is pleas - ant, Or bath - ing on the beach............ And
love to go to pic - nics, Or excursions down the bay............. To
when I'm think - ing of her I Can scarce - ly catch my
bug - - gy rid - - ing or fish - ing Is ve - - ry hard to
see all the styles of danc - ing, And hear the mus - ic
breath............ She came glid - - ing by so grace - ful, And so
beat............. But here's the best of all.... Some
played............ Each per - - son has their fa - vorite, But
hand - - some and so neat... ... That grace - - ful girl that
day I hope you'll meet............. That charm - - ing lit - - tle
mine is in - com - plete.. Un - til I meet that

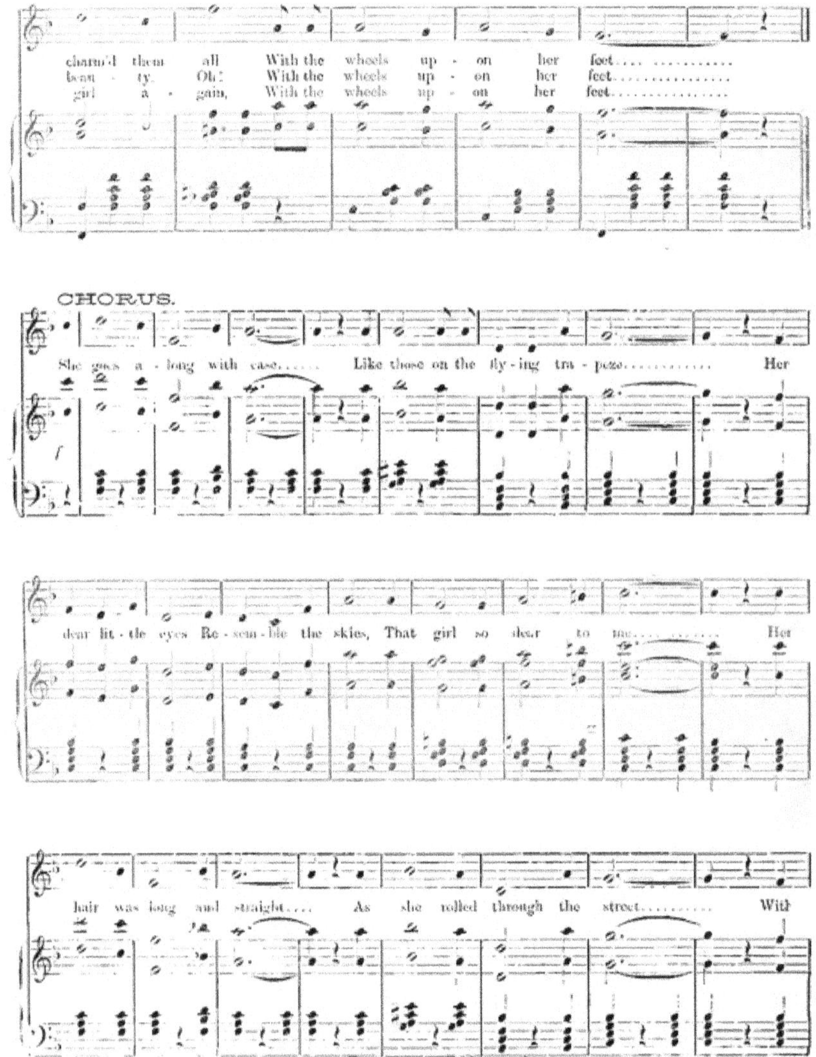
charm'd them all With the wheels up - on her feet....
beau - ty. Oh! With the wheels up - on her feet....
girl a - gain, With the wheels up - on her feet....
CHORUS.
She goes a - long with ease...... Like those on the fly - ing tra - peze.......... Her
dear lit - tle eyes Re - sem - ble the skies, That girl so dear to me........ Her
hair was long and straight.... As she rolled through the street........ With

wheels on her feet I thought I could eat, That girl on the roll - ing skates......
DANCE.

"FUN WITH THE BOYS."

SONG AND CHORUS.

Composed by G. R. LAMPARD.

1. No doubt you've heard the sto - ry oft, I'm go - ing to re - late, A -
2. There is a sto - ry go - ing round Which may have once been true, A -
3. The Par - son hur - ried on his way, But soon a form he met, With
4. The Par - son sees an - oth - er man, And hast - ens to his side, "They
4. This is the sto - ry oft - en told, And wheth - er right or wrong, When

bout a place not new, or old, Up in the Bad - ger State, Now
bout an Osh - kosh Par - - son And what came to his view, As
eyes "bugged" out and hat stove in, Whose clothes with blood were wet, "My
sure - ly have been kill - ing you." In tears the Par - son cried, "Oh
used so long to talk a - bout, Is just as well in song— And

do not laugh, or think me green, Don't make the slight - est noise, And
com - ing to the town one day, His "tracts" he soon de - stroys, When
friend" he says, where have you been? Your looks my faith de - stroys, Oh!
no, not much," just look you here, These are the kind of toys, An
if you don't be - lieve it And with sor - rows turned to joys, Just
I will tell you where to go............... To have some fun with the boys!
meet - ing a rough look - ing chap.............. Who'd been having fun with the boys!
I've just been up to Osh - kosh.............. To have some fun with the boys!
ear, a nose, a piece of scalp.............. When we have fun with the boys!
take a trip to Osh - kosh............. And have some fun with the boys!
CHORUS.
Soprano and Alto.
Hur - rah! for all the gal - lant boys, You meet through - out the
Tenor and Bass.
Piano.

west, They're brave and hon - est heart - ed lads And with good hu - mor
blest, But if you want some jol - ly fun, Mixed up with - out al -
- loys— Just take a trip to Osh - kosh And have some fun with the boys.

Fun with the Boys. Song. 3.

PRETTY LIPS

("NEUMY, NEUM.")

ARTHUR LLOYD.

1. I am a Bach - e - lor is - n't it sad, Lass - es ne'er lov - ed me,
2 Why is it oth - er men seem - eth so blest? Plen - ty of pret - ty girls,
3. Though not so good look - ing as when a lad, I'm not, at all ug - ly al -
4. Can I ask an - y girl pres - ent I see? To be so good as take

aint it too bad, Hun - dreds of pret - ty girls dai - ly I see,
pet - ted, ca - ress'd, Though I smile lov - ing - ly when them I see,
- though I look sad, My fig - ure's as good as a fel - low's can be,
pit - ty on me, An - swer, I'm wait - ing, for what will it be,

Yet there's not one of them will love me. There's a lit - tle beau - ty whom I
Yet there's not one of them will love me. But there's not a doubt that Mas - ter
Yet there's not an - y girl will love me. Why am I per - mit - ted like a
Yet there's not one of them will love me. Gra - cious good - ness what is in that
of - ten meet, She's such a dear, up - on my word I dote on her.
Cu - pid's dart, Has been fired by that fas - ci - nat - ing Mil - li - ner,
sim - ple flow'r? To with'r and die in all my bloom - ing youth - ful - ness,
makes me start She's o - ver there my pret - ty lit - tle Mil - li - ner,
She's a lit - tle Mil - li - ner in West Fifth street, Oh! would that she were
'Twas - n't meant for me but it has pierced my heart, Oh! would that she were
Would I were a fai - ry and pos - sessed the pow'r To call that char - mer
Sit - ting with a fel - low too, oh! my poor heart, I feel she ne'er be

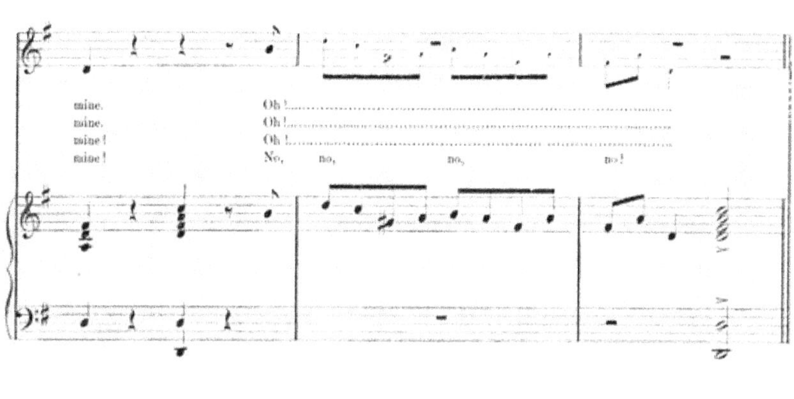
mine. Oh!
mine. Oh!
mine! Oh!
mine! No, no, no, no!

REFRAIN.

Pret-ty lips swee-ter than cher-ry or plum, Al-ways seem smil-ing, and nev-er look glum

Seem to say, "Come a-way, kiss-ie, come, come!" neum-y neum neum-y neum, neum, neum, neum!

MY LORD IS WRITIN' DOWN TIME.

JACOB J. SAWYER.

Piano.

MODERATO.
1. For He sees all you do, And He hears all you say, And my Lord is wri-tin' down time.......... He
2. Oh, He sees all you do, And He hears all you say, And my Lord is wri-tin' down time.......... He

sees all you do, And He hears all you say; Yes, my Lord is wri-tin' down time. Oh!
sees all you do, And He hears all you say; Yes, my Lord is wri-tin' down time. Oh!

Hal - le - lu - jah to de lamb! My Lord is wri - tin' down time, De Lord is in dere
Heben am a high and a loft- y place. My Lord is wri - tin' down time, And you'll go dere if

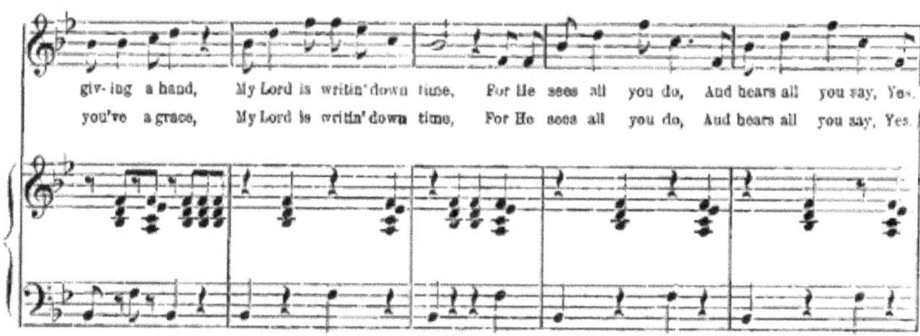
giv- ing a hand, My Lord is writin' down time, For He sees all you do, And hears all you say, Yes,
you've a grace, My Lord is writin' down time, For He sees all you do, And hears all you say, Yes,

my Lord is writin' down time..... He hears all you say, And sees all you do, Yes, my Lord am writin' down time

N 29 — 10

Sweet Kitty Clover.

Words by KNIGHT. Music by EDMUND KEAN.

Allegretto con espressione.
Piano.
1. Sweet Kit - ty Clo - ver she bothers me so.... oh...... oh......
2. Sweet Kit - ty, in per - son is ra - ther low... oh...... oh...... Sweet
3. Where Kit - ty re - sides I'm sure to go... oh...... oh...... Where
4. If Kit - ty to kirk with me would go... oh...... oh...... If
Sweet Kit - ty Clo - ver, she bothers me so... oh...... oh, oh........ Her
Kit - ty, in per - son is ra - ther low... oh...... oh, oh........ She's
Kit - ty re - sides I'm sure to go... oh...... oh, oh........ One
Kit - ty to kirk with me would go... oh...... oh, oh........ I

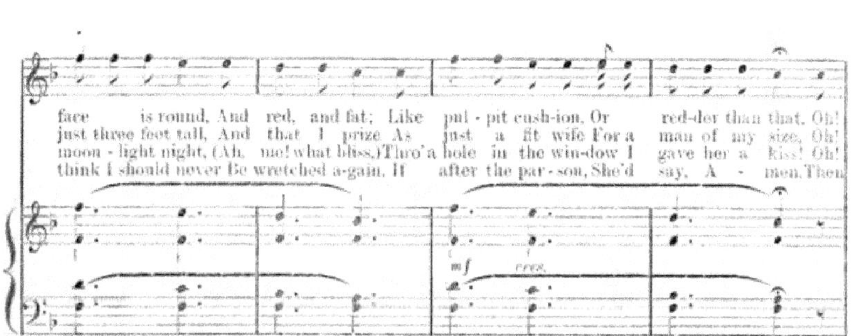
face is round, And red, and fat; Like pul - pit cush-ion, Or red-der than that, Oh!
just three feet tall, And that I prize As just a fit wife For a man of my size, Oh!
moon - light night, (Ah, me! what bliss,) Thro' a hole in the win-dow I gave her a kiss! Oh!
think I should never Be wretched a-gain, If after the par - son, She'd say, A - men. Then
mf
cres.

sweet Kit-ty Clo - ver, she both-ers me so... oh,.... oh,..... Sweet Kitty Clover, she
sweet Kit-ty Clo - ver, you both-er me so... oh,.... oh,..... Sweet Kitty Clover, you
sweet Kit-ty Clo - ver, you both-er me so... oh,.... oh,..... Sweet Kitty Clover, you
Kit-ty would ne'er a - gain both-er me so... oh,.... oh,..... Kit-ty would ne'er again
p

bothers me so,.. oh,.... oh, oh!....
both-er me so,.. oh,.... oh, oh!....
both-er me so,.. oh,.... oh, oh!....
both-er me so,.. oh,.... oh, oh!....
p
f

STOP THAT KNOCKING AT THE DOOR.

Words and Music by **A. F. Winnemore.**

Moderato.
1. I once did lub a col-ored Gal.......... Whose name was Su - zy
2. She was the prettiest yel-low Gal.......... That eb - er I did
3. Oh, de first one dat cum in de room, Was a dar - key dressed to
Brown, She came from old Vir - gin - ny, She was de fair - est in de
see, She neb - er would go walk - ing, Wid a - ny Col-ored man but
death, He looked just like de show - man What dey used to call Mack-
town; Her eyes so bright, dey shine at night When de moon am gone a-
me; And when I took my Ban - jo down, And played three tunes or
beth; He said he was a Cali - for - ni man, And just ar - rived on

way; She used to call dis dar-key up.......... Just a-fore de broke of
more; All at once I heard three pretty hard raps...... Come bang a - gain my
shore; I ax him whare-fore he cum an' rap So hard a - gainst my
day; Wid a who dar? who dar? who dar? An' a who dar a knocking at my
door.
door.
(Spoken. Why, Sam!)
door? Am dat you Sam? am dat you Sam? No you bet-ter stop dat knocking at my
(Spoken. Aint you gwan to let me in?)
By Bass Voice.
door? Let me in. Stop that knocking. Let me in. Stop that knocking. Let me in.

DUET.
1st Voice.
Oh! you bet - ter stop that knock-ing at the door. Stop that
Bass.
Oh! I'll nev - er stop that knocking at the door. Let me in.
knocking. Stop that knocking. Oh, you bet-ter stop that knocking at the door.
Let me in. Let me in. No, I'll nev-er stop that knocking at the door.
CHORUS.
1st & 2d Voices.
Stop that knock-ing, stop that knock-ing, stop that knock-ing, stop that knock-ing, Oh! you
Tenor.
Stop that knock-ing, stop that knock-ing, stop that knock-ing, stop that knoc-king, Oh! you
Bass.
No I'll

bet - ter stop that knocking at my door, Stop that knocking, stop that knocking, stop that
nev - er stop that knocking at your door, Let me in. Stop that knocking, stop that knocking, stop that
knocking, stop that knocking, Oh! you bet - ter stop that knocking at my door.
knocking, stop that knocking. No! I'll nev - er stop that knocking at your door.
8va
8va

To Miss FLETA M. HOLMAN.

MARGARETHA.

C. L. JENKS, JR.

INTRODUCTION.
legato.
p
pp

mf
1. Sinks the sun in o-cean's
2. On the rock my head re-
mf
rit.
p
mf

flow - - ing, Shines the sky in la - test glow - - ing;
-clin - - ing, Strang - er in a strange land pin - - ing,

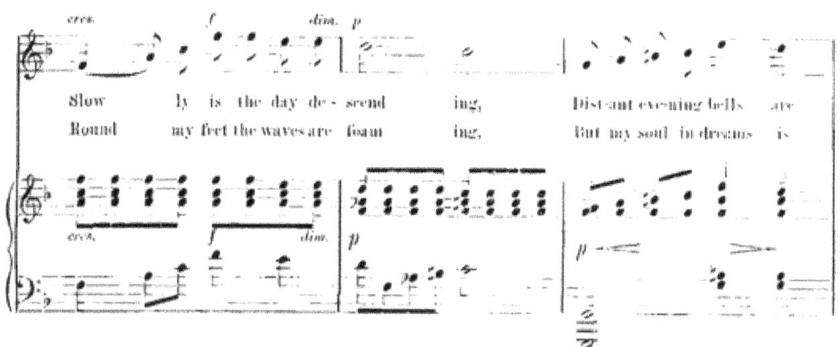
cres.
f
dim.
p
Slow ly is the day de - scend ing,
Dist-ant evening bells are
Round my feet the waves are foam ing,
But my soul in dreams is
cres.
f
dim.
p
p

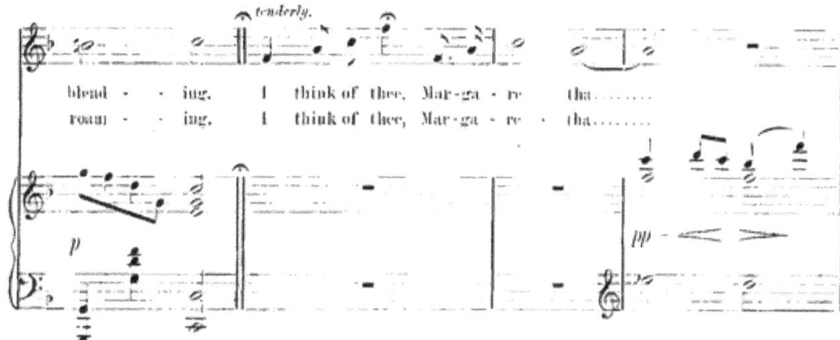
tenderly.
blend - - ing. I think of thee, Mar-ga - re tha.......
roam - - ing. I think of thee, Mar-ga - re - tha........
p
pp

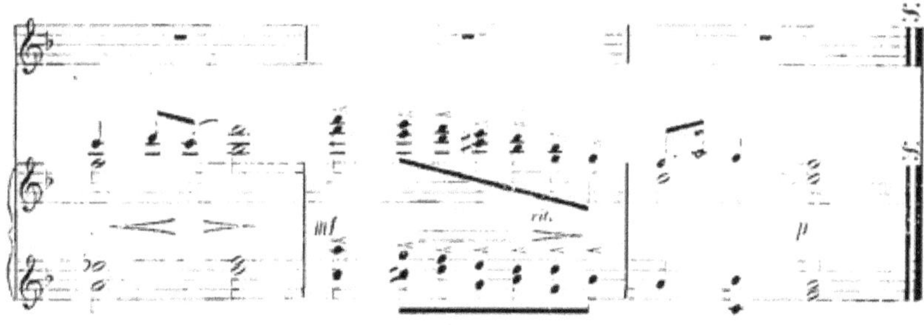
mf
rit.
p

You'll Sometimes Think of Me.

By CHARLES COOTE, Jr,

p
rit.
1. The days are past, the time gone by, Since
2. In time to come, what - e'er be - tide. Where
p

first I - breath'd to thee, Those ten - der words of
ev - er you may be, Though bound - less o - cean
love and truth, When yet thine heart was free, But
roll be - tween, My thoughts will be with thee, And
now stern fate our sep' - rate paths, Had traced with harsh de -
though all joys of life may cease, When you no more I

-cere, My on - ly hope is still that you, Will
see, My fer - vent trust will still be that, You'll
some - times think of me, My on - ly hope is
some - times think of me, My fer - vent trust will
still that you, Will some - times think of me.
still be that, You'll some - times think of me.
f

CHORUS.
SOPRANO.
You'll some-times think of me, You'll some-times think of me. My
ALTO.
TENOR.
You'll some-times think of me, You'll some-times think of me, My
BASS.
PIANO.
on - ly hope is still that you, Will some-times think of me.
on - ly hope is still that you, Will some-times think of me.

MAMMA'S CHILD.

A CRADLE SONG.

Words and Music by GEORGE M. CARLETON.

Allegretto.
rall.
p
1. Mam - ma's child is tir - ed now, And read - y for her bed, . . . She
2. Morn - ing breaks, the child a - wakes, And o - pens her blue eyes, . . . She
3. Sit - ting by the old log fire To - day she's sweet six - teen, . . . Oh,
takes her gent - ly on her knee, And good - night pray'rs are said, . . . When
tot - ters o'er to mam - ma's bed, To kiss her then she tries, . . . Then
back - ward turn ye years of flight, Make me a child a - gain, . . . That

mam - ma lays her in her crib, Her gol - den curls she strokes . . Of
with her toys she plays all day, Till eve - ning's dusk has come, . . . With
I may hear my moth - er sing, Her nurs - 'ry rhymes to me, . . . As
all the treas - ures in this world My child I love thee most. . . . .
tir - ed limbs and sleep - py eyes, To mam - ma she will run. . . . .
hap - pi - ly I'm rock'd to sleep, Up - on her dear old knee. . . . .
rall.

Refrain.

Slum - ber on my dear, . . With - out care or fear, . . And the cra - dl

gent ly swings too and fro, . . . For mam - ma's close by, . . .
colla voce.
And if ba - by cries, She will then sing to her so soft and low.
Chorus.
Bye, bye ba - by hunt - ing, Pa - pas gone a hunt - ing,
p
rit. dim.

www.ingramcontent.com/pod-product-compliance
Lightning Source LLC
Chambersburg PA
CBHW020555270326
41927CB00006B/846

* 9 7 8 3 7 4 4 7 8 4 3 7 5 *